O. F. E...

D0518020

CANDLELIGHT VIGIL, SEPTEMBER 12, 2001.

For those who lost their lives on September 11, 2001,
the Star-Spangled Banner waves in honor and hope.
To them we dedicate this book.
And in their names we send this message to the world:
Our hearts have been broken;
our spirit has not.

LINCOLN MEMORIAL, WASHINGTON, D.C.

FIRES ENGULF THE WORLD TRADE CENTER, SEPTEMBER 11, 2001. OVERLEAF: MORE THAN 16,000 FORM A HUMAN FLAG AT TUCSON ELECTRIC PARK, SEPTEMBER 15, 2001.

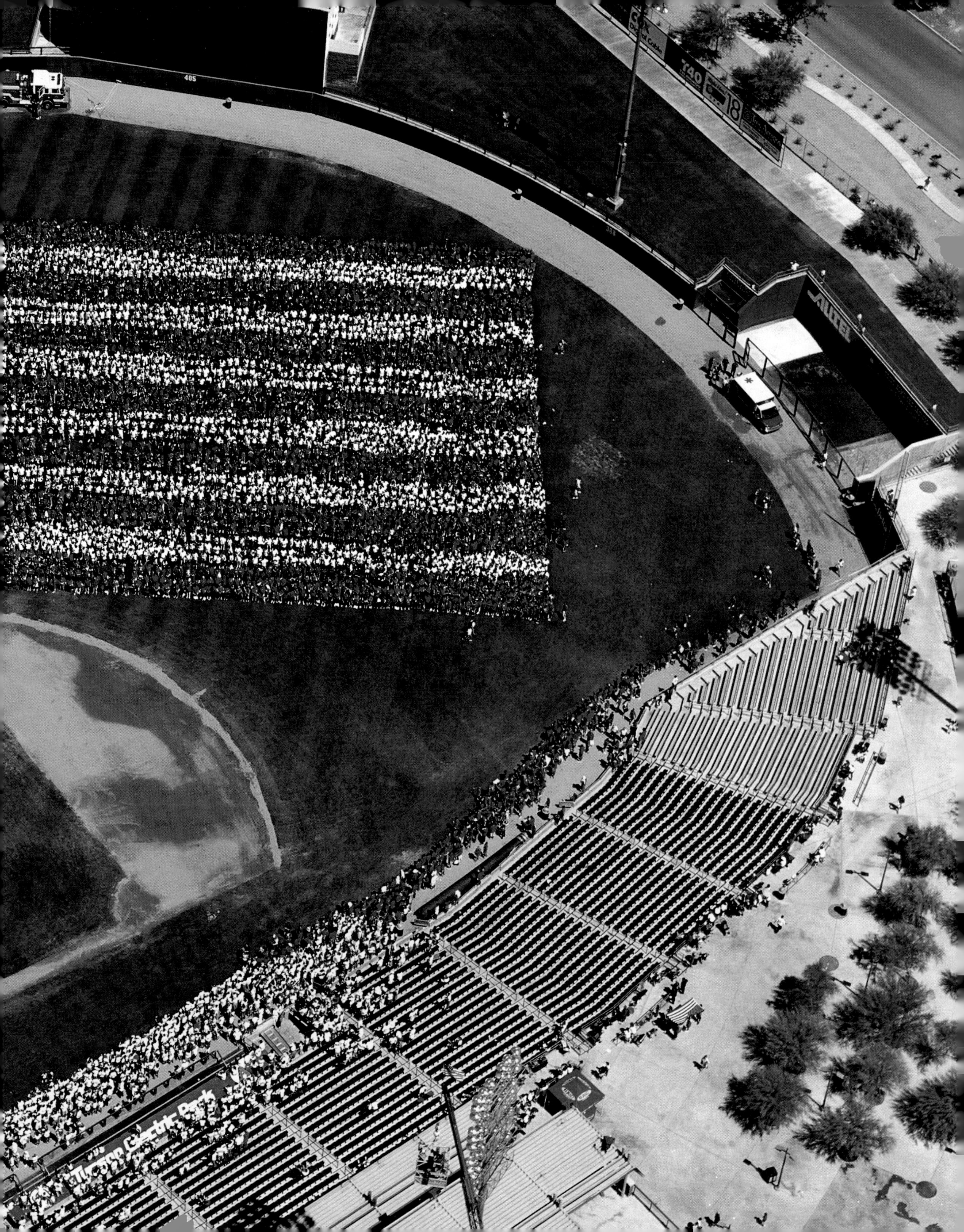
405
740
18

An American flag is posted in the rubble of the World Trade Center, September 13, 2001.

MOURNERS AT A MEMORIAL FOR WORLD TRADE CENTER VICTIMS IN NEW YORK CITY'S UNION SQUARE PARK, SEPTEMBER 18, 2001.

THE PENTAGON, SEPTEMBER 16, 2001.

A FUNERAL PROCESSION IN NEW YORK CITY FOR FIREFIGHTER LT. DENNIS MOJICA. OVERLEAF: SCENE OF DEVASTATION AFTER THE WORLD TRADE CENTER COLLAPSE, SEPTEMBER 11, 2001.

STAR-SPANGLED BANNER

BANNER

Our Nation and Its Flag

BY MARGARET SEDEEN

PREPARED BY THE BOOK DIVISION

NATIONAL GEOGRAPHIC SOCIETY, WASHINGTON, D.C.

Foreword

By Douglas Brinkley

Preceding Pages: Old Glory spans an area of Central Park on Flag Day, 1981.

Overleaf: Cadets display the flag at a University of Michigan football game.

S trange now to remember how I used to take the American flag for granted. It was omnipresent but never truly understood. Like most Americans I would stand at attention and sing Francis Scott Key's national anthem at ball games, use the flag as a podium prop in my classroom, or feel good about seeing the red, white, and blue displayed fashionably every Fourth of July. It was such a familiar icon, in fact, that it became invisible and uncontemplated. True, there was something reassuring about seeing the flag wave above car dealerships and fast-food joints, but it offered no dazzle or meaning. It was a blasé symbol that life in the United States was business as usual.

All those sentiments evaporated on September 11, 2001, when two jetliners, one American, one United, crashed into the World Trade Center, an American Airlines plane struck the Pentagon, and a United flight burst into flames in a Pennsylvania field. More than 5,000 were killed in the most ghastly terrorist attack in American history. As TVs across the land replayed ad nauseam footage of the destruction, a collective silence blanketed households from Maine to California. Scoundrels had punctured the post-Cold War myth of American invincibility. Everyone understood that we would never be the same again. For a few hours we were paralyzed with fear and grief. Would there be more attacks? Who committed this horrendous deed? Why didn't the CIA prevent the sneak attacks? Our first instinct was to connect with loved ones to make sure they were safe. Telephone switchboards lit up like Christmas trees. If you knew anyone in New York or Washington, D.C., you were anxious for confirmation that they were out of harm's way. Once that reassurance arrived, we all calmed down and wondered what to do next. That is when the miracle of America occurred.

Spontaneously a wave of patriotism unseen since World War II fanned out across our nation. As our confusion lifted and the dark cloud of hate dissipated, pride swelled inside our body politic and came bursting forward in the ubiquitous display of the Star-Spangled Banner. Within hours, Wal-Marts and mom-and-pop stores sold out of flags. From closets, trunks, and garages families dredged out Old Glory to fly in their front yards. Radio stations played

Lee Greenwood's anthem "I'm Proud to be an American" with pronounced regularity. Decals were slapped on car bumpers and office windows. Red-white-and-blue ribbons were even worn by objective TV anchors.

The Star-Spangled Banner was everywhere. It felt almost unpatriotic not to be wearing or waving or singing about the flag. With this spontaneous eruption of sentiment came the miracle: Overnight the gruesome images of the World Trade Center in ruin were countered by a blast of patriotism. Slogans like "United We Stand" and "God Bless America" appeared on billboards and T-shirts with the flag as a backdrop. The ever-so-familiar object spoke to our hearts, hopes, and aspirations. This was not a battle flag in the war against terrorism, but a symbol of peace and unity in a world of chaos, a world gone wrong. It reminded us of sacrifice past, of George Washington's troops freezing at Valley Forge, of men losing limbs and life at Iwo Jima. John F. Kennedy's famous oration, "Ask not what your country can do for you but what you can do for your country" became the prevailing ethos as volunteerism flourished. Citizens queued up at Red Cross stations to give blood, or eager college students signed up at their schools' ROTC offices, ready to help fight what President George W. Bush called "The War Against Terrorism." In a novelty gesture, Great Plains farmers painted their livestock red, white, and blue. More than 16,000 citizens formed a human flag at Tucson Electric Park. Trucks roared down the highways, flags waving from their antennas. People turned on their computers to find e-mail messages about duty, honor, country, flag. Reminiscent of World War II, everyone understood that "We are all in this together."

And suddenly, in the midst of one of our nation's greatest tragedies, we felt good about ourselves. Words like freedom and democracy and justice flowed from our lips with revitalized conviction. Skyscrapers may have tumbled, but, as Key wrote during the crucible of the War of 1812, "our flag was still there" —everywhere. As tributes to our martyred dead proliferated, the Postmaster General even issued a special American Flag stamp to further remind us of our shared tradition.

Now, like most of my fellow citizens, I no longer see the flag as a mere object. It is a Great Spirit that embodies the aspirations and dreams of our forefathers. In those giant Star-Spangled Banners that hung from the Pentagon and the World Trade Center after the attacks, there was life that no suicidal coward could ever pierce. The entire drumbeat of our history resonates in those 50 stars, which now blaze brighter than ever. The names of the recent dead will live on in the impenetrable fabric of the cloth we cherish so deeply.

We honor the victims of terrorism by honoring Old Glory.

Table of Contents

Introduction

I t is the lifeblood of our nation . . . the Star-Spangled Banner . . . Old Glory . . . the Stars and Stripes . . . the Red, White, and Blue . . . . How does a piece of cloth come to hold such power?

Perhaps most simply, the American flag carries an encoded picture of our past and our present. Its 13 stripes signify the original 13 colonies, its 50 stars the 50 states. It portrays our country's beginning and its growth. But it is so much more.

The flag is the single symbol that bonds the diverse United States. It stands for the land and the people, the government, and the nation's ideals. It embodies the heroism of Americans both famous and anonymous, our identity as a people, our dreams of the future.

Every wave of the flag is a pulse of history, a commemoration of multitudes of real, tangible, concrete events all melded into a single, grand, abstract concept: America. The American flag has been called the object of a national love affair and cited as the symbol of a civil religion. Indeed, some scholars claim that Americans feel a veneration for their flag far beyond that of citizens of any other nation. This observation would come as no surprise to most Americans. Even those who do not share the feeling are aware that the symbolism of the flag resonates throughout American life.

And Americans have not been shy about their civil religion, which endows our national symbol with religious significance. In 1864, as Abraham Lincoln placed Ulysses S. Grant at the head of the Union Army, a Pennsylvania patriot spoke of the American flag's "sacred Past" and "Heaven-ordained Future." In the autumn of 1917, as American troops rushed to France to support Allied forces in World War I, the NATIONAL GEOGRAPHIC magazine published a "Flag Number." The issue, distributed free by the thousand

Edward Percy Moran's "By Dawn's Early Light" (opposite), painted in 1912, depicts that legendary moment on the morning of September 14, 1814, when Francis Scott Key and his compatriots Col. John Skinner and Dr. William Beanes spy the American flag waving above Baltimore's Fort McHenry. Inspired by the sight—a sign that the night-long British attack had failed—Key composed his famous ode to that symbol of American freedom and bravery, the Star-Spangled Banner.

A mid-1800s portrait of a youthful patriot clutching an early version of the Stars and Stripes personifies the freedom and the hope promised by the young Republic. The democratic ideal continues to draw immigrants, such as the Yen Dinh family (opposite), who escaped from Vietnam by boat. Pictured at journey's end, after the parents' naturalization ceremony at Thomas Jefferson's Monticello on the Fourth of July, the new Americans proudly display their allegiance to their adopted country. For the occasion, Mrs. Dinh made flag-inspired dresses for her daughters.

to the United States Army and Navy, opened with the statement that "the flag epitomizes for an army the high principles for which it strives in battle." The text warns that the flag keeps ideals ever before the soldier. If it were not for the flag, the soldier "would be bestialized by slaughter." The flag, said the magazine, keeps the fighting man "eager for personal sacrifice in the cause."

Why does the flag have this power? Because, asserted Editor Gilbert Hovey Grosvenor, its "origin is divinity itself." Grosvenor is echoed almost a generation later, on the eve of World War II, by retired U. S. Army Col. James A. Moss, who cites the same source as Grosvenor: the Book of Genesis, 9:13, which describes the first flag. It was the firmament-wide, many-colored banner of the rainbow, which, God said to Noah, was "a token of a covenant between me and the earth."

Americans follow the flag that waves at the head of a parade with a fervency akin to that in the hearts of marchers bearing holy icons in old Russia. In 1828, President-elect Andrew Jackson proclaimed that in a perfect democracy "the voice of the people is the voice of God." Some 130 years later, writing from his Birmingham, Alabama, jail cell, Martin Luther King, Jr., said that civil rights protesters were defending America's "most sacred values . . . those great wells of democracy which were dug deep by the founding fathers."

Sentiments such as these span our nation's history and are part of what the flag represents. It carries our image of ourselves as a chosen people, as inhabitants of what is still, in many ways, a brave new world. The idea of America as a utopia fired the imagination of European explorers. When they looked this way they saw a land that seemed, in the words of 16th-century French Huguenot colonizer Jean Ribaut, "the fairest, frutefullest and plesantest

of all the worlde." The English seafarer Francis Drake, in the summer of 1579, found in California "a goodly country and fruitful soil, stored with many blessings fit for the use of man." It was the search for such blessings—and for freedom—that drew the first settlers to the shores of North America. Today the same search brings to the United States immigrants who, as new citizens, pledge allegiance to the flag of red and white and blue.

Contrary to popular belief, there is nothing "official" to explain the significance of the colors. The human compulsion to invest colors with meaning—usually abstract qualities, virtues, and ideals—is ancient and universal. Thus it might be expected that one of the myths clinging to the story of the American flag is that George Washington, at some uncertain time, ascribed to the red our inheritance from Great Britain and to the white a representation of liberty. In this pretty story, Washington is ambiguous on the matter of the blue, but later multitudes have not been. The blue has been said to symbolize justice, faith in God, loyalty, friendship, truth. To the color red have been given courage, zeal, and "the life blood of brave men and women." The white has been assigned purity in word and deed, "cleanness of life and rectitude of conduct." The purpose of these claims seems didactic, their goal to set forth for Americans a pattern for patriotic living and to sanctify the flag as the very substance of American heroism. They speak with the voice of established authority.

It is no wonder, then, that outrage met the long-haired counterculture of the 1960s and its appropriation of the flag to convey its own message, its challenge to authority. By the late sixties, the Vietnam War had become a focus of protest not only by counterculture Americans, but also by many in the mainstream. On college campuses and city streets, young people marched, chanted, burned draft cards—and burned the American flag. Often they put the Stars and Stripes to uses both unconventional and defiant. Many Americans asked: Should the flag be used as a tool to shock society? Whose flag is it, anyway?

Some answers to that question came in the summer of 1991. A group of 20 men and women, supported by a caravan of motor homes, ran a nonstop relay, carrying the American flag more than 3,000 miles from San Francisco to Washington, D. C. The flag they handed from one to another some 900 times was not the 13-stripe, 50-star flag we now see every day. Their flag bore 15 stripes and 15 stars. It was a replica of the flag that flew over Baltimore's Fort McHenry during the War of 1812, the flag that inspired Francis Scott Key to write "The Star-Spangled Banner," designated by Congress in 1931 as our national anthem.

The runners ran their relay to spread the word of a project to honor Key and "The Star-Spangled Banner." Their aim was to arouse national interest in the Star-Spangled Banner Monument, to be built by the Francis Scott Key Foundation in Washington, D. C., on a site only a few paces from where Key's home stood at the time that he wrote the national anthem.

The 18-day relay passed through desert, mountains, and plains. Crowds greeted the runners with cheers, banners, and praise. As part of the group took a break in St. Louis, a waitress told them: "This kind of thing gives me

The Washington Monument obelisk (opposite) soars behind a windblown Stars and Stripes. Legend ascribes the meaning of the flag's colors to George Washington. In actuality, the nation's chief symbol has no inherent meaning. Thus, depending on the viewer's perspective, the flag may paradoxically signify patriotism or protest, as it did during the 1960s. Above, a young hippie conveys her cause for peace with flag and candle in San Francisco's Golden Gate Park.

In the early 1800s, when Francis Scott Key (above) sat for portraitist Joseph Wood, the Maryland-born attorney figured actively in church and civic affairs around fashionable Georgetown, where he lived with his family (opposite). Key had moved to the capital in 1805 to take over his uncle's law practice. His causes célèbres included a winning defense plea in the Supreme Court hearing for the accomplices of accused traitor Aaron Burr. An advocate for Negroes' rights, Key lobbied for the abolition of slavery. In 1833, with his appointment as U. S. District Attorney for the District of Columbia, he left Georgetown for the less charming quagmire of Washington City.

faith in the country." The runners carried their Star-Spangled Banner to the Gettysburg Battlefield, to the Liberty Bell in Philadelphia, to Fort McHenry, to the Vietnam Veterans Memorial in Washington, and finally onto the grounds of the Francis Scott Key Memorial Park in Georgetown.

Just to the west of today's park site and the busy Key Bridge, which crosses the Potomac River, stood the house where Francis Scott Key lived from 1805 to about 1833 with his wife, the former Mary Tayloe Lloyd of Annapolis, Maryland, and their six sons and five daughters. The house was demolished in 1947, after years of neglect by various owners, but there exists a painting of it as remembered by Key's grandson John Ross Key. The scene is one of tranquility and prosperity. In it, a large, handsome brick house sits amid leafy trees on what seems to be a quiet lane, although Georgetown at the time was a snug, thriving town of some 5,000 people only a few miles from the Capitol, the White House, and other federal buildings of Washington City. A small annex to the house serves as Key's law office. In the painting, guests are arriving at the front door—a woman with a child by the hand, perhaps a playmate of the Key children. In a letter to his grandmother, Key described the family home: "The shady lawn and orchard sloping to the Potomac's edge, and the terraced garden with its lofty Walnut trees and Lombardy Poplars shading the walks, make a happy playground for the household band."

In August 1814 it was not a happy playground. On the evening of the 24th, after a day on horseback rushing to and fro as aide to a militia general, Francis Scott Key sat with his family in their house, windows bolted tight in spite of the summer heat. British troops had invaded and captured Washing-

ton. They had set fire to the Capitol and the White House. Through most of the night the flames shone as far away as Baltimore, 40 miles from the federal city. Only the rains of a dawn thunderstorm kept the fires from spreading.

British soldiers and fleeing Washingtonians jammed the roads. The next day, more buildings were burned—and a second thunderstorm with heavy rain again dampened the fires. Their work done, the British troops marched back to their ships in and about the Chesapeake Bay.

A few stragglers from the British forces found themselves in the village of Upper Marlboro, in the Maryland countryside. Stories vary as to their motives and conduct. Were they unruly looters? Were they only begging food and water? At any rate, they entered the house of the distinguished elderly town physician, Dr. William Beanes, who was celebrating a false

Kenneth Townsend's rendering of the British bombardment of Fort McHenry on September 13-14, 1814—the last time it would come under enemy fire—reveals the strategic setting of the Baltimore garrison. The site, which occupies the point of a peninsula along the Patapsco River, was first fortified with the building of Fort Whetstone in 1776. At the turn of the century, it was replaced by Fort McHenry, a pentagonal structure designed by French engineer Jean Foncin and named for then Secretary of War James McHenry.

Based on a design first conceived in the 16th century, the star-shaped fort provided the last line of defense against a land attack. With no blind spots, soldiers could protect every wall. Should enemy soldiers penetrate the two lines of harbor defense—first, the shoreline guns and second, the dry ditch—they would have to face defending soldiers stationed with cannon or muskets at each point, or bastion.

Fort McHenry holds the unique designation of national monument and historic shrine.

19

This engraving depicts the death of Maj. Gen. Robert Ross on September 12, 1814. As the British commander, surrounded by his advance guard, moved into Baltimore for a simultaneous land-and-sea strike on the city, two local boys, so the story goes, shot and killed the officer. The following day British land troops, now under the command of Col. Arthur Brooke, attempted to take the city, while the navy, under Adm. Sir Alexander Cochrane, shelled Fort McHenry. The surprisingly strong American defense, composed mainly of the Baltimore militia, convinced the British officers to retreat on September 14.

report of an American victory with friends. The merrymakers escorted the stragglers to the village jail. The news reached the British commander, Gen. Robert Ross, who sent a detachment back to Upper Marlboro to arrest Beanes and two other offending Americans. Beanes's confederates were soon released, but the doctor was detained aboard the British flagship, *Tonnant*.

In the days following the attack on Washington, as American forces readied for the assault on Baltimore that they knew would come by both land and water, friends of Dr. Beanes's made an appeal for help in securing his freedom. It was the popular and respected 35-year-old Georgetown lawyer, Francis Scott Key, who came to their aid.

On September 2, Key wrote to his mother, "I am going in the morning to Baltimore. . . . Old Doct. Beanes of Marlboro is taken prisoner by the enemy, who threaten to carry him off. . . . I hope to return in about eight or 10 days, though it is uncertain, as I do not know where to find the fleet."

Aboard a sloop flying a flag of truce approved by President James Madison, Key set sail from Baltimore with Col. John Skinner, an American agent for prisoner exchange. On September 7, they sighted and boarded the *Tonnant* to confer with General Ross and Adm. Alexander Cochrane. At first, the two refused to release Dr. Beanes. Then Key and Colonel Skinner produced their trump card—a pouch of letters from wounded British soldiers whom Ross had left behind, in praise of the care they were receiving from the Americans, among them, Dr. Beanes. Although Ross and Cochrane then relented, the letters did not secure immediate freedom for Beanes and his rescuers.

Because Key and Skinner had spent so much time aboard ship among the British, they were aware of plans for the impending attack on Baltimore. A smiling Admiral Cochrane said to Skinner, "You could hardly expect us to let you go on shore in advance of us." The British moved the three Americans, under guard, to the sloop on which they had arrived and forced them to wait out the battle from behind the British fleet.

On shore stood the star-shaped Fort McHenry. An American flag had been ordered for the fort in the summer of 1813, when a marauding British fleet had appeared in the Chesapeake Bay. The fort's commander, Maj. George Armistead, had asked for a flag so big that, in his words, "the British will have no trouble seeing it from a distance." Armistead wanted a "suitable ensign," a clear signal of American resolve. Two officers, a commodore and a general, went to the Baltimore home of Mary Young Pickersgill, a "maker of colours," and commissioned the flag. In her upstairs front bedroom, Mrs. Pickersgill and her 13-year-old daughter Caroline went to work. They used 400 yards of best quality wool bunting, at least some of which Mrs. Pickersgill herself may have woven. They cut 15 stars that measured two feet from point to point. They cut stripes—eight red and seven white—each two feet wide. To lay out the flag and sew it together, they used the malthouse floor of a neighboring brewery. By August the "suitable ensign" was finished. It cost $405.90 and measured 30 by 42 feet.

Now, a year later, the new flag was ready to greet the enemy. Early in the morning of September 13, the British bombardment fleet began to maneuver, sometimes coming as close as a mile and a half from the fort, sometimes

O say can you see, ~~through~~ by the dawn's early light,
What so proudly we hail'd at the twilight's last gleaming,
Whose broad stripes & bright stars through the perilous fight,
O'er the ramparts we watch'd, were so gallantly streaming?
And the rocket's red glare, the bomb bursting in air,
Gave proof through the night that our flag was still there,
O say does that star-spangled banner yet wave
O'er the land of the free & the home of the brave?

On the shore dimly seen through the mists of the deep,
Where the foe's haughty host in dread silence reposes,
What is that which the breeze, o'er the towering steep,
As it fitfully blows, half conceals, half discloses?
Now it catches the gleam of the morning's first beam,
In full glory reflected now shines in the stream,
'Tis the star-spangled banner — O long may it wave
O'er the land of the free & the home of the brave!

And where is that band who so vauntingly swore,
That the havoc of war & the battle's confusion
A home & a Country should leave us no more?
— ~~Their blood~~
Their blood has wash'd out their foul footstep's pollution.
No refuge could save the hireling & slave
From the terror of flight or the gloom of the grave,
And the star-spangled banner in triumph doth wave
O'er the land of the free & the home of the brave.

O thus be it ever when freemen shall stand
Between their lov'd home & the war's desolation!
Blest with vict'ry & peace may the heav'n rescued land
Praise the power that hath made & preserv'd us a nation!
Then conquer we must, when our cause it is just,
And this be our motto — "In God is our trust,"
And the star-spangled banner in triumph shall wave
O'er the land of the free & the home of the brave. —

THE STAR SPANGLED BANNER.

Published by John Cole, Baltimore.

CON SPIRITO

The handwritten draft of Francis Scott Key's untitled poem (opposite), now preserved at the Maryland Historical Society, reveals the national anthem in its earliest form. Key wrote the verse to fit the tune of "To Anacreon in Heaven"—a popular song whose melody provided a vehicle for numerous, often patriotic, American and British songs.

Thomas Carr, an English immigrant and music publisher based in Baltimore, printed the first sheet music for "The Star-Spangled Banner." Credit, however, often goes to his friend John Cole—another English music publisher in Baltimore—who, in 1822, purchased some of Carr's plates and stock. Around 1825, Cole published his edition of the song (left).

moving back out of range of the American guns. The British ships fired bombshells that weighed 200 pounds and carried lighted fuses supposedly measured to explode the shell when it reached its target. But these bombs were undependable devices and often blew up in midair. From a specially designed ship and from small boats, Cochrane's men fired rockets that traced wobbly arcs of red flame. In the evening the cannonading stopped, but about one o'clock in the morning, on the 14th, the British fleet again roared into action, lighting the rainy night sky with grotesque fireworks.

With Colonel Skinner and Dr. Beanes, Francis Scott Key watched the battle, by day with a spyglass, by night with apprehension. As long as the bombardment continued, they knew that Fort McHenry had not surrendered, but early in the morning, long before daylight, there came a sudden and mysterious silence. No bombs burst. No rockets blazed. What the three Americans did not know was that the British land assault on Baltimore, as well as the naval attack, had been abandoned. Judging Baltimore too costly a prize, the British officers had ordered retreat.

In the predawn dark, Key waited for the one thing that would end his anxiety. That would be the joyous sight of Major Armistead's great red,

The flag that flew at Fort McHenry (opposite)—now a remnant measuring 30 by 34 feet—today hangs in the Smithsonian Institution's Museum of American History. The origin and significance of the mysterious red "V" on one of the white stripes remain unknown.

Exactly what happened to the flag through the night at Fort McHenry is still in question as well. A British midshipman's account published in 1841 describes the triumphant hoisting of a huge flag over the fort as the British withdrew. Quite possibly during the rainy, windswept night, unbeknownst to Key, a similar but smaller storm flag had been substituted to protect the larger Stars and Stripes.

To guard the fragile cloth from light and dust, an opaque curtain shields the flag, which is only exposed for viewing every 60 minutes during museum hours.

white, and blue flag blowing in the breeze above the fort just as it had the evening before. At last, daylight came. The flag was still there.

Key, long an amateur poet, knew that this was the time for brave verses. On the back of a letter he had in his pocket, he began to write. Sailing back to Baltimore he composed more lines, and in his hotel he finished the poem. One of his friends took it to a printer, and soon, as a broadside, it was circulating around Baltimore under the title "Defence of Fort M'Henry." Local newspapers printed it, then papers as far away as Georgia and New Hampshire. To the verses was added the note, "Tune: Anacreon in Heaven." This was a popular English drinking song that Key himself had used before, when he composed a poem in honor of Stephen Decatur's feats in the Barbary Wars. In October a Baltimore actor sang Key's new song in a public performance and called it "The Star-Spangled Banner."

Over the years our response to the flag has remained, for the most part, constant—we have looked to it with reverence, pride, and joy. In other ways, as this book will show, our feelings have been as confused as some of the paths we have taken as a nation.

On these pages you will follow rebellious colonists who defied British rule and humanitarians who brought aid to Somalia. From the Revolutionary and Civil Wars to Vietnam and beyond, you will witness heroes who carry the flag into battle and statesmen who stand by it on missions of foreign diplomacy. Through the story of the Star-Spangled Banner, you will journey with trailblazers as they explore their own land, the world, and space itself. You will also see Americans at home, at work, at school, in politics and sports, and discover the rich heritage of our nation's most enduring symbol.

The Birth of the Flag

In December 1606 three small ships of the Virginia Company of London set sail down the Thames. The *Susan Constant, Godspeed,* and *Discovery* all flew white banners, each with a bold red cross. From the mainmast of the *Susan Constant,* the largest of the three vessels, yet another flag fluttered, a bright tumble of darting lines and angles of red, white, and blue. Great storms and contrary winds held the ships in the English Channel. Only after "six weekes in the sight of England" were they able to brave the Atlantic Ocean and bear toward their destination along the eastern coast of North America.

The Virginia colony founded in May 1607 by a few score planters—the "adventurers" were those who stayed home and ventured capital—was named Jamestown for James I, the English king who had given them their charter as a joint-stock company. Jamestown, although it suffered many disasters, was the first successful English settlement in North America.

The white banner bearing the red cross was known as the flag of St. George. It had been an English national flag since the Middle Ages, when, with other western Christians, English Crusaders under Richard I and Edward I had set out to wrest the Holy Land from Muslim powers. In the city-state of Genoa, the English armies fell under the spell of the fourth-century martyr St. George, whose miraculous intervention as a valiant knight was credited with many a Christian victory. A 13th-century manuscript related that at the 1099 siege of Jerusalem, the figure of the saint appeared, clad in his familiar white armor emblazoned with a red cross, and exhorted the Englishmen to climb the scaling ladders. By 1415 the Archbishop of Canterbury called St. George the "patron and special protector" of England.

A mid-19th-century wood engraving illustrates American celebrants at New York Harbor on November 25, 1783 (opposite), when the last British troops evacuated the city. As a parting gesture, the troops left behind their flag, which they nailed to a flagpole at Fort George in the Battery. To make its removal even more challenging, they detached the halyards and greased the staff. A ladder solved the problem, allowing a nimble American to tear down the British Union Jack and raise the Stars and Stripes, accompanied by a 13-gun salute.

In May 1497, John Cabot set out from England to explore the north-eastern coast of North America for Henry VII, with the king's authority to display "our banners and ensignes." A century later, Sir Francis Drake, circumnavigating the world in his famous flagship, the *Golden Hind,* anchored off the coast of what is now California and named the country New Albion, in honor of an ancient name for England. A period map of Drake's voyage shows the flag of St. George planted on New Albion, marking this English claim in the New World.

John Cabot, his son Sebastian, and Drake all had special permission to fly, along with the red cross, the royal standard—the king's own flag—with its heraldic devices from France and England.

The Jamestown flagship, *Susan Constant,* flew a third banner in addition to two flags of St. George. This was a flag whose design would endure in America well into the Revolutionary War. It was created after the death of Elizabeth I in 1603. The Scottish king, James VI, had been asked to take the throne and so became James I of England. To give the ships of the united England and Scotland a proper ensign, in 1606 James proclaimed: "from henceforth all our subjects of this Isle and Kingdom of Great Britain . . . shall bear in their maintop the Red Cross, commonly called St. George's Cross, and the White Cross [of Scotland], commonly called St. Andrew's Cross, joined together." In 1625, in the list of flags raised at James's funeral, this was called "the Banner of the Union." Thus it became the Union flag or, simply, the British flag.

The founders of the Massachusetts Bay Colony also sailed into the New World under the cross of St. George. It was there, in the settlement of Salem in 1634, that the earliest known flag desecration on American shores

took place. The staunch Puritan leader John Endecott expressed his disapproval of non-Puritan ways and devices—from the Anglican Book of Common Prayer to the ancient maypole dance. He did not like the cross on the flag because, as Governor John Winthrop explained, "the red cross was given to the king of England by the pope, as an ensign of victory, and so a superstitious thing, and a relique of antichrist." Endecott ordered the cross to be cut away from Salem's flags. Many leaders of the Massachusetts colony thought the action a rash and dangerous defiance of royal power, and Endecott received an official rebuke.

Even so, Puritan hostility to the symbol was so great that flags bearing the cross of St. George were shot at and were scarce in the colony for decades to come. As late as 1680, Dutch visitors to the town of Boston observed that the flag flew without the red cross. One exception had been made. In 1651 the General Court of Massachusetts permitted the cross to

Godspeed, Susan Constant, and Discovery, rendered by Lt. Cmdr. Griffith Bailey Coale in 1949 (above), approach the Virginia coast at Jamestown in 1607. The European use of crosses, either worn on surcoats or carried as pennants, as emblems of quick identification in war and peace, and on land and at sea, began with the Crusaders, or "cross-bearers." Those crosses directly related to the history of the American flag include (opposite, top to bottom) the English St. George's Cross, the Scottish St. Andrew's Cross, and the British, or Union, flag.

fly over a royal fort in Boston Harbor on the grounds that "the old English colors now used by the Parliament" were "a necessary badge of distinction betwixt the English and other nations in all places of the world, till the state of England alter the same, which we very much desire." The court also prudently recognized that the fort was the property of the crown.

In 1649, King Charles I, son of the Scottish James, lost his head, a victim of the civil war. Scotland and England broke apart, and Parliament decreed that "the Ships at Sea in service of the State shall onely beare the red Crosse in a white flag." By 1660, upon the restoration of the monarchy under Charles II, the Massachusetts Council of State ordered that "Standards, flags and Jacke Colours for the ffleete be forthwith prepared as were in use before 1648."

In the harbors of the American Colonies, British ships flew flags of many varieties. A jack flag is one that usually flies from the bowsprit, and in design resembles the national flag. Early jacks were small Union flags. Later, British ships flew a jack with a red field and the cross of St. George or the Union crosses in the canton—the upper corner of the flag nearest the staff. This was known as a British red ensign. Another flag, that of the British East India Company, bore a striking similarity in design to the flag that would be flown by the Colonies early in the Revolutionary War and the flag that evolved into the Stars and Stripes—the Continental Colors. Possibly known to American merchant seamen, the East India Company flag had red and white stripes, usually 13, and the Union Jack in the canton.

Regional feelings grew among the American colonists and found expression in local flags. By 1700, Massachusetts had added a pine tree to the red cross in the canton of the colony's flag, placing it in the upper corner nearest the staff. Because the field of this flag was red, it has also been called a red ensign.

Why a pine tree? Perhaps because—ever green and evoking immortality—it already carried a connotation of place and culture, of individuality, of differences between Englishmen in England and Englishmen in America. The symbol had been used on the pine tree shilling, a silver coin minted in Boston from 1652 to the early 1680s.

An ornate Massachusetts flag, and the oldest existing flag in the United States, is the Bedford flag. Made—probably in England in the 1660s—for the combined militias of three Massachusetts counties, the Bedford flag is a square of crimson damask. Painted in black and silver on the field is a bent arm clad in armor, extending from a cloud and holding a sword—an "arm of God." A gold ribbon bears the words VINCE AUT MORIRE—Conquer or Die. The flag is now preserved in the Bedford Free Public Library.

The motif that appealed most widely to the American colonists was the snake. Perhaps its earliest venture into American politics was in Benjamin Franklin's *Pennsylvania Gazette* of May 9, 1754. Here was a drawing, possibly Franklin's own handiwork, entitled JOIN, or DIE. It showed a snake severed into segments, each bearing the name of a colony, and above the snake's head, the label "N. E.," for the New England colonies. Franklin's purpose was to promote his Plan of Union to bring together the Colonies—which would retain individual sovereignty— under "one general government." Both the British government and the

The use of ensigns in the early 1600s marked a major change in British flag design. Variations of the red ensign—the pictured version (opposite, top) features a Union Jack—appeared for some 150 years on ships, forts, and in military formations. The striped flag of the East India Company (bottom) incorporated a St. George's Cross, perhaps as early as 1616. Evidence indicates that the company may have replaced the canton's cross with the Union in keeping with a royal decree in 1707.

Overleaf: Col. John Trumbull's "The Battle of Bunker's Hill," painted in 1786 by the Revolution's main documentary artist, depicts the death of physician and patriot Joseph Warren on June 17, 1775. Trumbull's eyewitness account includes the 1686 New England pine tree ensign. The conspicuous omission of the St. George's Cross may signify an oversight or a rebellious colonial gesture—that is, if the flag actually flew at all. Some historians think this improbable and attribute its presence here to artistic license.

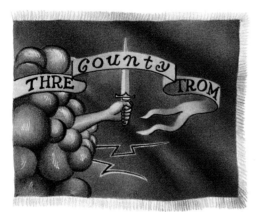

Colonial flags displayed symbols of individualism and the frontier. This English-made, red damask banner (above, left) represented the Three County Troop, a Massachusetts Bay cavalry company. The allegorical design—used in Holland and Poland, and by both sides in the English civil war of 1642-46—reappears in the Bedford flag (above, right). A cornet about two feet square, this flag is thought by some to have flown at the Battle of Concord on April 19, 1775.

The snake (opposite), an ancient symbol of wisdom, appeared in a cautionary cartoon in Benjamin Franklin's Pennsylvania Gazette *in 1754. Used as a flag motif during the 1770s, it evolved into a rattlesnake. During the Revolution it became a popular emblem of the United States, as seen in the Gadsden Standard, with its yellow field, and the striped Navy jack.*

Colonies eventually rejected the plan, but the ideas of colonial cooperation and autonomous rule led to the formation of the Continental Congress—the body that governed the Colonies during the Revolutionary War.

A citizen of Philadelphia had contemplated the qualities of the rattlesnake. Satisfied that it was a proper American symbol, and fortuitously native to the New World, he took only slight liberty with fact, and wrote: "I recollected that [the rattlesnake's] eye excelled in brightness, that of any other animal, and that she has no eye-lids—She may therefore be esteemed an emblem of vigilance. She never begins an attack, nor, when once engaged, ever surrenders: She is therefore an emblem of magnanimity and true courage. . . . [Her] wounds however small, are decisive and fatal:—Conscious of this, she never wounds till she has generously given notice, even to her enemy, and cautioned him against the danger of treading on her. . . . I confess I was wholly at a loss what to make of the rattles, 'till I went back and counted them and found them just thirteen, . . . and I recollected too that this was the only part of the Snake which increased in numbers—. . . . One of those rattles singly, is incapable of producing

JOIN, or DIE.

DONT TREAD ON ME

DONT TREAD ON ME

sound, but the ringing of thirteen together, is sufficient to alarm the boldest man living."

The letter, signed AN AMERICAN GUESSER, was published in the *Pennsylvania Journal* on December 27, 1775. Recently the scholar and editor J. A. Leo Lemay identified the witty American Guesser. He was Benjamin Franklin.

Soon the snake device had become unquestionably a rattlesnake and had evolved from a symbol of colonial division to one of defiant unity. Military units from Pennsylvania and Rhode Island carried flags showing a coiled rattlesnake and the warning DONT TREAD ON ME. Such a flag, in 1778, went with a combined colonial land force under Gen. John Sullivan to besiege Newport. In 1776 a yellow flag that bore an ominous dark rattler ready to strike was flown as a personal flag by Esek Hopkins, the commander of the tiny Continental Navy. The Navy ships also carried the Continental Colors as a national flag.

British troops based in Boston had harassed the locals for many months. Massachusetts militia and minutemen prepared for war, conducting drills and stockpiling ammunition. At dawn on April 19, 1775, some 700 British soldiers advanced on Lexington and Concord to destroy American munitions and supplies. At the Battle of Concord, minutemen from nearby

In W. J. Edward's engraving (opposite, top), a company of minutemen crossing Concord's North Bridge with a Massachusetts pine tree ensign dispute and deter British troops after the battle at Lexington on April 19, 1775. The British meant to destroy the cache of powder and arms at Concord and to arrest colonial leaders. Massachusetts flew the pine tree at sea, accompanied by the colony's motto (opposite, bottom).

Born between the hostilities at Lexington and Concord and the Declaration of Independence, the Grand Union flag (above)—unofficial in design and designation, and subject to variation—became known as the first national colors of the United States.

Bedford followed their flag, with its arm of God and its motto, "Conquer or Die." In June, colonial forces built fortifications near Bunker Hill in an attempt to dislodge the British Army from Boston, across the river. At this battle, one of the bloodiest of the Revolution, the Americans flew the New England pine tree flag and, although beaten by the British, came to regard the outcome as a moral victory that quelled tales of Yankee cowardice.

American stripes began to appear about this time. The British called them "the rebellious stripes." One famous flag, dating from 1775 or 1776, is known as one of the first Colonial Navy jacks. This jack shows a rattlesnake, its tongue flicking as it runs across a field of red and white stripes that varied in number. The words DON'T TREAD UPON ME curve along the serpent's body.

The Colonies, by mid-1775, had determined to raise an army. On June 15, the Continental Congress appointed George Washington its commander. By autumn 1775, George Washington had commissioned a small number of ships, under army command, to intercept British supply boats on their way to Boston. Col. Joseph Reed wrote to the men outfitting the fleet: "Please to fix upon Some particular Colour for a Flag—& a Signal, by which our vessels may know one another—What do you think of a Flag with a White Ground, a Tree in the Middle—the Motto (Appeal to Heaven)—This is the Flag of our floating Batteries." But the letter was tardy, and the ships sailed under their old flags, probably the Continental Colors, although, as Reed explained, the pine tree identified the cannon-bearing scows known as floating batteries.

By the end of 1775, Washington had assembled only a few thousand

diverse and poorly committed troops, but on January 1, 1776, the day the Army's existence became official, the Americans raised the Continental Colors on a tall pole on Prospect Hill near Boston and Washington's Cambridge encampment. Three days later, referring to a copy of a recent speech by King George III, Washington wrote to his friend and secretary, Lieutenant Colonel Reed: "We are at length favored with the sight of his Majesty's most gracious speech, breathing sentiments of tenderness and compassion for his deluded American subjects; the speech I send you (a volume of them was sent out by the Boston gentry), and farcical enough, we gave great joy to them without knowing or intending it, for on that day which gave being to our new army, but before the proclamation came to hand, we hoisted the union flag in compliment to the United Colonies. But, behold! it was received at Boston as a token of the deep impression the speech had made upon us, and as a signal of submission."

Soon after, a British sea captain wrote home from Boston: "I can see the Rebels' camp very plain, whose colours a little while ago were entirely red; but on receipt of the King's speech (which they burnt) they have hoisted the Union Flag, which is here supposed to intimate the union of the provinces."

The red flag sighted on Prospect Hill by the British officer was a liberty flag. It flew from a staff known as a liberty pole. After the passage of the Stamp Act in 1765, liberty poles, liberty flags, liberty trees, and the radical patriot groups called Sons of Liberty had become focal points of colonial resistance throughout the Colonies.

In Boston, the Sons of Liberty gathered under a great elm tree. This was the first liberty tree, and from its branches hung effigies of many a despised royal official. High above the branches, from a pole affixed to the trunk, often fluttered a red flag as a summons to the citizenry to gather around the latest handbill preaching discontent and insurrection. In 1775 the fate of the elm was described by the *New England Chronicle*: "The enemies of liberty and America, headed by Tom Gage [the royal governor], lately gave a notable specimen of their hatred to the very name of liberty. A party . . . repaired to a tree at the south end of Boston, known by the name of 'Liberty Tree,' and, armed with axes, &c., made a furious attack upon it. After a long spell of groaning, swearing, and foaming with malice diabolical they cut down a tree because it bore the name of 'Liberty.'"

In Charleston, South Carolina, patriots assembled under a live oak. When a copy of the Stamp Act reached Charleston, according to flag historian George Henry Preble, a group of men "captured the paper" and "displayed a flag showing a blue field with three white crescents." Later, in 1775 and 1776, South Carolina forces flew a blue flag with a silver or white crescent in its upper corner. The South Carolina patriot William Henry Drayton described the flag that flew over a fort in Charleston Harbor as blue "with a white crescent; on which was emblazoned the word 'Liberty.'"

Liberty flags were as diverse as the Colonies, yet spoke in a single voice. In New York a liberty pole flew what Preble called "a splendid flag," bearing the words "The King, Pitt, and Liberty," in thanks to William Pitt, the British prime minister who had promoted repeal of the Stamp Act. Some liberty poles carried the striped Continental Colors with that ubiquitous motto. Some are thought to have flown a flag with nine red and white vertical stripes and a rattlesnake. Sometimes the flag was a red ensign. When the British marched on Concord, one of their lieutenants

Clyde de Land's painting (opposite) depicts the raising of the Continental Union flag on Prospect Hill by George Washington's new Continental Army, a consortium of local colonial units. The event signified more than a local protest: Chosen as representatives of the 13 Colonies, these soldiers from Massachusetts acted on behalf of all the Colonies, hence in the name of America.

The artist may have inaccurately included George Washington as the figure on horseback. Most historians agree that Washington was not present at the flag raising.

John C. McRae's engraving, after a painting by F. A. Charman, depicts colonists cheering at the raising of a liberty pole to show their dedication to freedom and their opposition to tyranny. In New York, after the British destroyed two such liberty poles, the Sons of Liberty erected a third with an iron-sheathed base. It stood for three years. When that pole too was torn down, city officials refused to allow another one to be raised on public ground. After July 4, 1776, flags on the liberty poles represented the new union of American states.

reported that they took a hill "with a liberty pole on it and a flag flying which was cut down," although he did not describe the flag. In August 1776, on Long Island, Hessian mercenaries captured 11 American flags, all proclaiming "Liberty."

The truest parent of the Stars and Stripes was a flag of 13 red and white stripes with the British Union in the canton. This is known variously as the Grand Union flag, the Great Union flag, the Continental flag, and the Continental Colors. Historians agree that the design of the Continental Colors reflected two ideas. First, the 13 stripes represented the Colonies, unified and aggrieved. Second, the inclusion of the Union demonstrated that the colonists were still loyal subjects of King George, though sorely tried by laws that the British Parliament aimed at American coffers and the American citizenry.

By July 1776 the colonists had declared their independence, announced that "Life, Liberty and the pursuit of Happiness" were God-given rights of all men, and named their new country the United States of America. A new country would seem to need a new flag, but there was no great hurry about getting one. The business of war was more urgent. Almost a year later, in spring 1777, a committee of Congress met to plan defenses against an expected British attack on Philadelphia, to seek means of obtaining foreign aid and advice, to appropriate money, and to consider naval appointments. At the June 14 session a simple statement quietly and without elaboration made its way into the record: "Resolved, That the flag of the thirteen United States be thirteen stripes alternate red and white; that the union be thirteen stars, white in a blue field, representing a new constellation."

A new constellation. A stellar configuration suddenly arisen in the heavens, somehow an emblem of the fledgling, self-made United States? What did the Congress mean by a "new constellation"?

No one knows. Neither the Congressional resolution nor any known document of the time addressed the arrangement of the stars, nor does anything explain why, in the first place, stars were chosen. And, unless some long-lost, definitive record, such as a letter or a diary, comes to light, we will never know.

Theories have not been scarce. For instance, the stars stand for "lofty aspirations." Or: The star, as a symbol of Freemasonry, would have appealed to Washington, Franklin, and other members of the secret society. And: The constellation was Lyra—to signify harmony. It is true that Rhode Island military units, early in the war, carried flags with 13 stars in the canton and, on a white field, a blue anchor with the words IN GOD WE HOPE. However, exact dating of those Rhode Island flags has been impossible. They may have come before the June 1777 flag resolution but, equally, they may have followed its example.

In 1927, discussing the flag of 1777, historian John Spargo wrote, "Every American boy and girl before graduating from the primary school learns the story of Betsy Ross and how she made, and helped to design, the first Stars and Stripes flag." This may have been true in 1927. It is not true today, nor was it true before the late 19th century, when William J. Canby—Mrs. Ross's grandson—declared that in childhood he had heard the story from the lips of the lady herself.

As Canby told it in 1870, reading a paper before the Historical Society of Pennsylvania, General Washington and two representatives from

A variety of symbols decorated liberty banners throughout the 13 Colonies during the mid-1770s. Col. William Moultrie's liberty crescent (opposite, top), designed "for the purpose of signals," was the first American flag flown in South Carolina. Colonists in Taunton, Massachusetts, raised this version (opposite, bottom) of a union flag.

Line officers presented this starred Rhode Island regimental flag (above), one of two versions, to the General Assembly of Rhode Island on February 28, 1784.

Congress appeared on Mrs. Ross's doorstep around the first of June 1776. They asked that she make an American flag according to a sketch they carried with them. At Mrs. Ross's suggestion, Washington modified the flag design "in her back parlor" to employ stars of five points instead of six. Canby's paper and sympathetic affidavits from other relatives constitute the only affirmation of the story, while the facts of history deny it.

For one thing, the date of the visit was Canby's guess because he knew that Washington had been in Philadelphia in early June. But this was a month before the Declaration of Independence—before there even was a United States. In 1777 the flag resolution itself re-declared independence by removing the British Union from the American flag. Also, while there had been requests for regimental and naval flags on the part of officials from General Washington on down—in fact, Betsy Ross had been paid in May 1777 "for making ship's colours" of an unknown design for Pennsylvania—few Americans seemed to expect a national flag until 1777 and later.

The Betsy Ross story gradually assumed in the popular mind the power of myth. In this myth, Betsy Ross presides as midwife at the birth of an idea conceived by the Father of our Country. However, careful historians have never accepted it. Spargo did not. Preble, who corresponded with Canby, did not. Most writers ever since have either ignored the story or challenged it. Betsy Ross has been cloaked in mystery, as have so many people and events of the past. Our colonial ancestors were not favored, as we are today, with a frenetic press corps whose job it is to witness, probe, and record every event of every day. At the same time, there often seems to be a wistful regret, best expressed, perhaps, by President Woodrow Wilson when asked his opinion of the story. He replied, "Would that it were true!"

In 1780 a claim was made to Congress by Francis Hopkinson asking payment for having furnished designs for government documents, seals, and "the flag of the United States of America." Hopkinson was a popular patriot, a member of the Continental Congress, a signer of the Declaration of Independence, a lawyer, poet, and artist. John Adams, in a letter to his wife, Abigail, described an encounter with Hopkinson in the studio of the Philadelphia painter Charles Willson Peale. Hopkinson, said Adams, "is one of your pretty little, curious, ingenious Men. His Head is not bigger, than a large Apple. . . . I have not met with anything in natural History much more amusing and entertaining, than his personal Appearance. Yet he is genteel and well bred, and is very social." But Hopkinson's prestige and general popularity were not enough to prevail over the congressional committees that considered his applications, first to be paid with "a Quarter Cask of the public wine" and later for $1,440 in Continental paper. After many months Congress rejected the charges but did not dispute Hopkinson's role. They said only that other men too had been "consulted."

Just because there was, after June 14, 1777, an official United States flag, no one should assume that the country's flags suddenly achieved uniformity. Word of the new design spread slowly. Also, in a small, poor nation fighting for its life, the making of new flags was not easy. The Continental Colors, as well as state flags, continued to fly on

The legend of Betsy Ross, apocryphal maker of the first Stars and Stripes, is interpreted here in Elisabeth Moore Hallowell's 1896 drawing (opposite, top). A few years earlier another artist, Charles E. Weisgerber, painted Ross's alleged meeting with a committee of Congress, inventively rendering her flag with a circular star pattern (bottom). Exhibited at the 1893 Columbia Exposition in Chicago, the much-seen painting only further mired the story in myth.

Among those who contributed to the design of the Stars and Stripes, signer of the Declaration of Independence and artist Francis Hopkinson (above) may have borrowed the idea of stars for the flag from his star-studded coat of arms.

Scottish-born patriot John Paul Jones, portrayed by Ferdinand de Brackeleer, cuts a valiant figure with cutlass and pistol before an idealized Stars and Stripes (right). Before his departure from Portsmouth, Virginia, in November 1777, the captain of the Ranger received news of the congressional resolution to substitute stars for the Union in the Continental Colors. The day he sailed into Quiberon Bay, France, on February 13, 1778, at least two different flags waved from the ship. One likely featured horizontal stars in a 4-5-4 pattern and 13 red, white, and blue stripes (opposite), and the other a pattern of red and white stripes.

Navy ships after the resolution. In August 1777 at Fort Schuyler, in New York's upper Mohawk Valley, Americans prepared for a British attack. One officer wrote later that the fort had never had a flag and described the common desire for one as the enemy approached. The men made themselves a flag by cutting white stripes from ammunition shirts, blue stripes from a wool cloak captured from the British, and red stripes from "different pieces of stuff collected from sundry persons." In other words, not yet the Stars and Stripes.

When 13 stars did appear on American flags, they were arranged in a variety of patterns. The flag thought by some to have flown in August 1777, when Americans routed the British at Bennington, Vermont, has one star in each upper corner of the canton, with eleven stars in a spacious semicircle that arcs above the number 76, to commemorate the year of independence. There were stars in circles, stars in rows of varying numbers, stars forming larger stars. The number of star points varied. Matters were confused even further in 1778 when an ambassador from the Kingdom of the Two Sicilies asked about the American flag; Benjamin Franklin and John Adams wrote in reply that it had "thirteen stripes, alternately red, white, and blue" and thirteen white stars "denoting a new constellation."

According to 19th-century historian George Bancroft, as Philadelphia celebrated the first anniversary of the Declaration of Independence, "bells rung all day and all the evening; ships, row-galleys and boats showed the new Flag." The Stars and Stripes received its first foreign salute on February 14, 1778, the morning after John Paul Jones sailed the *Ranger* into Quiberon Bay, in France. Following a protocol quibble over the number of guns with which the French flagship would return the American 13-gun salute, Jones, desirous of the foreign recognition, accepted 9 guns instead of the 11 he had hoped for.

Thirteen stripes and thirteen stars, perfect symbols of the United States in 1777, were by 1794 no longer representative. In 1791, Vermont had become a state, and 1792 saw Kentucky's statehood. The next year the Senate easily passed a bill increasing the flag's stars and stripes to 15. When the bill came before the House of Representatives, much windy debate ensued. Arguments of those in favor ranged from a desire to broadcast to the world word of the new states to a desire to pass the bill and get it over with. Opponents called the bill frivolous and protested that new flags would cost $60 apiece for every ship in the country. Benjamin Goodhue of Massachusetts cautioned that making this change would mean altering

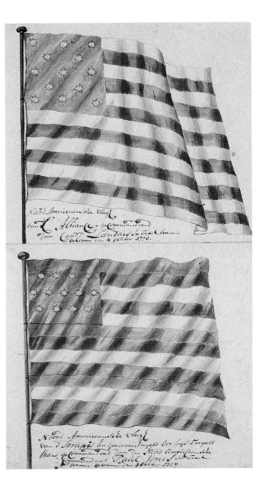

Streamers of light ignite the sky above Independence Hall, birthplace of the Constitution, as Philadelphians celebrate the Fourth of July. The city threw its grandest, most exuberant party here for the nation in 1876, the year of the Centennial—a time to reflect on and take pride in the century's progress, to reaffirm faith in democracy, and to mend rifts. The country went all out to mark its 100th birthday with the staging of the Centennial Exhibition in Philadelphia's Fairmount Park. The extravagant climax on July 4 included a parade attended by notables from around the world, a reading of the Declaration of Independence, speeches, and a grand finale of fireworks, torch lighting, and bell ringing.

The Stars and Stripes: Variations on a Theme

The ambiguous wording of the Congressional flag resolution of June 14, 1777—which established the flag's elements but neglected to specify their design—coupled with the slow dissemination of the news, inspired an array of "official" versions of the Continental Colors. The examples above have all been claimed as Revolutionary relics.

Clockwise from top left: The Schuyler flag, said to be Gen. Philip Schuyler's New York headquarters flag of 1777, features a circle of five-pointed, hand-appliquéd cotton stars. Its machine-stitched stripes and heading, however, give it away as a mid to late 19th-century piece.

Oral history alone dates the Guilford Court House or North Carolina militia flag to the Revolutionary battles of the Carolinas. Unique in its colors and dimensions, this flag, now a fragment, probably had at least fourteen stripes

and perhaps two more eight-pointed stars on the left.

Although some claim that this flag was flown at the Battle of Bennington on August 16, 1777, the actual age of the now faded banner, with its seven-pointed stars, has not been proven. Nevertheless, every August 15 through 17 since 1963, local Vermonters have raised the Bennington Battle colors at the statehouse to commemorate their victory.

Its 13-star pattern and the reversed position of its stars and stripes support claims that the Easton flag, a silk standard from Pennsylvania, predates the flag resolution of 1777. Documents trace it to September 6, 1814, when it was presented to a local militia unit called up for the War of 1812. As local legend has it, however, it was displayed during the public reading of the Declaration of Independence on July 8, 1776.

the flag repeatedly as the country grew. By a vote of 50 to 42, the House passed the bill. It stipulated that after May 1, 1795, "the flag of the United States be fifteen stripes, alternate red and white; and that the union be fifteen stars, white in a blue field." This was the flag that flew on American ships during hostilities with France from 1798 to 1801. In 1803 it was raised over New Orleans after the Louisiana Purchase. It was the flag carried on the western explorations of Lewis and Clark and Zebulon Pike. Fifteen stars and fifteen stripes flew over Fort McHenry during the War of 1812, and became Francis Scott Key's "Star-Spangled Banner."

But Benjamin Goodhue's warning had been a wise one. In 1796, Tennessee joined the Union; in 1803, Ohio; in 1812, Louisiana. In 1816, Indiana became a state. By now there were 19, with Mississippi soon to come. Here and there around the country, flags went their own way. Over one government building in Washington, D. C., there was a flag with only 9 stripes. The Navy Yard's flag had 18. Vermont flew a flag with 17 stars and 17 stripes. Louisiana had one with 18 of each. A Congressional committee, directed by New York's Peter Wendover, studied the problem for many months and, early in 1818, presented a report. The committee had heard arguments against increasing the number of stripes in the flag. Naval officers claimed that the American flag of 13 stripes was more easily identified at sea. Most people recognized that it was foolish to consider adding more and more—narrower and narrower—stripes. Wendover had sought the advice of Samuel

Thure de Thulstrup's 1906 painting details the lowering of the French flag and the raising of the American colors on December 20, 1803. The ceremony, held in a public square in New Orleans, signaled the transfer of Louisiana by Napoleon to the United States—an acquisition that more than doubled the country's territory at a cost of $15 million.

*Reminiscent of the "new constella-
tion" born in the nation's struggle
for independence, a modern Stars
and Stripes—measuring 20 by 30
feet—appears to emanate from the
Star of Destiny, a crystal set in the
high, light-studded ceiling of the
Shrine Room in the Indiana World
War Memorial in Indianapolis.*

Chester Reid, a naval captain and hero of the War of 1812. It was Reid's view that the 13-stripe flag honored the original Colonies and that new states could be honored by the relatively simple addition of stars. Reid's view prevailed in the House and the Senate.

On April 4, President James Monroe signed into law the Flag Act of 1818. It read:

> **Section 1.** Be it enacted, &c., That from and after the fourth day of July next, the flag of the United States be thirteen horizontal stripes, alternate red and white; that the union have twenty stars, white in a blue field.

> **Section 2.** And be it further enacted, That on the admission of every new State into the Union, one star be added to the union of the flag; and that such addition shall take effect on the fourth of July next succeeding such admission.

And the flag as we know it today was born. Almost. The committee had not specified the arrangement of the stars. While President Monroe preferred them in rows, Congress, in a most independent American fashion, had left the pattern flexible, "whether in the form of one great luminary [a star shape], or, in the words of the original Resolution of 1777, 'representing a new constellation.'"

The United States of America began to take its place on the world stage. The mysterious words were prophetic—a new constellation was indeed ascendant on the horizon.

The Flag in War and Diplomacy

The Flag in War and Diplomacy

The roots of American nationalism are old and deep. Long before the Revolutionary War, colonists spoke of "American patriots," "my country," and "our nation." By the mid-18th century, the diverse Colonies, though often in disagreement, were well acquainted with one another. They fought together in the French and Indian War, a conflict most knew was—in Benjamin Franklin's words—"really a British war." In 1782, French immigrant Jean de Crèvecoeur wrote, "The American is a new man," but, in many ways, he had been a new man from the day he entered the New World.

The colonists rebelled when King George III decided that they should bear more of the cost of Britain's American empire. The new enforcement of trade laws began to restrict colonists who had happily accustomed themselves to smuggling. The crown levied taxes on newspapers, documents, glass, lead, paper, and tea. Warships and troops arrived in Boston, where three regiments of redcoats paraded with fife and drum and colors flying.

Eventually Parliament repealed all the taxes but one, and tea became "the beverage of traitors" and the food of fishes at "tea parties," most notably in Boston. In 1774, when Parliament punished Massachusetts by closing the port of Boston, other Colonies sent food—from Carolina rice to bleating flocks of Connecticut sheep.

On May 10, 1775, the same day that the Second Continental Congress assembled in Philadelphia, a colonial force under the command of Ethan Allen and Benedict Arnold surprised a sleeping Fort Ticonderoga and captured its wealth of artillery—which the next winter Col. Henry Knox dragged by a 42-sled ox train all the way to Washington's army near Boston.

United States Marines risked their lives to raise the Stars and Stripes atop Mount Suribachi during the battle for Iwo Jima, one of World War II's bloodiest fights. The struggle for the rugged, fiercely defended island cost the lives of 5,931 U. S. Marines, including three of the six who carried the flag to the summit. Their heroic effort, captured by a press photographer, became a symbol of American determination and courage.

Mocking England's Stamp Tax with a macabre parody, the Pennsylvania Journal *notified readers that the paper would cease publication rather than pay the tax. Britain's levy on newspapers and documents, imposed in 1765, caused angry American colonists to unite against their mother country.*

Threatened by a hostile mob in Boston on March 5, 1770, frightened British troops fired their muskets into the crowd, killing five people. The soldiers were acquitted of murder, but patriots used Paul Revere's misleading print of "the bloody massacre" (opposite) to inflame the colonists.

Fort Ticonderoga's cannon, among other things, convinced the British to withdraw from Boston in the spring of 1776 and turn their attention toward New York. By the end of the year, American armies abandoned their Hudson River forts. Washington's troops retreated across New Jersey—in the general's words, a "melancholy situation." The British settled into their winter quarters, leaving Hessian mercenaries to guard Trenton. Again hauling Henry Knox's cannon, Washington and his men surprised the garrison and captured it, along with horses, guns, musical instruments, and a thousand prisoners. It was the day after Christmas, 1776. In a few victorious days early in the New Year, Washington regained most of New Jersey, a feat that boosted American morale.

Baron von Steuben, the Marquis de Lafayette, the Polish patriot and engineer Tadeusz Kosciuszko, and other Europeans arrived to serve with Washington. The French, eager to help rupture the British Empire, secretly sent generous aid to the American army including arms, clothing, gunflints, and powder. What eventually convinced France—and Spain and the Netherlands—to make open alliances with the colonists was the American victory over the British general John Burgoyne at Saratoga in October 1777.

The war soon took a decisive turn south. Savannah fell to the British late in 1778, and Charleston in the spring of 1780. In October 1780, American frontiersmen defeated the British at King's Mountain, South Carolina. Three months later, in a woodsy Carolina pasture known as Cowpens, a Continental army under Daniel Morgan, with William Washington, a cousin of the commander in chief, routed a British army led by a cavalryman famous as "Bloody Tarleton." Morgan's brilliant victory

THE BLOODY MASSACRE perpetrated in King——Street BOSTON on March 5th 1770 by a party of the 29th REGT.

Engrav'd Printed & Sold by PAUL REVERE BOSTON

Unhappy BOSTON! see thy Sons deplore,
Thy hallow'd Walks besmear'd with guiltless Gore:
While faithless P——n and his savage Bands,
With murd'rous Rancour stretch their bloody Hands;
Like fierce Barbarians grinning o'er their Prey,
Approve the Carnage, and enjoy the Day.

If scalding drops from Rage from Anguish Wrung,
If speechless Sorrows lab'ring for a Tongue,
Or if a weeping World can ought appease
The plaintive Ghosts of Victims such as these;
The Patriot's copious Tears for each are shed,
A glorious Tribute which embalms the Dead.

But know, FATE summons to that awful Goal,
Where JUSTICE strips the Murd'rer of his Soul:
Should venal C——ts the scandal of the Land,
Snatch the relentless Villain from her Hand,
Keen Execrations on this Plate inscrib'd,
Shall reach a JUDGE who never can be brib'd.

The unhappy Sufferers were Messrs. SAML GRAY, SAML MAVERICK, JAMES CALDWELL, CRISPUS ATTUCKS & PATK CARR

Killed. Six wounded; two of them (CHRISTR MONK & JOHN CLARK) Mortally

Col⁰ by C⁰ T Remich

The Flag in War and Diplomacy

ultimately forced the British general Charles Cornwallis into Virginia to the small tobacco port of Yorktown.

At Cowpens, Morgan captured at least two British flags—the king's standard and the colors of the Seventh Fusiliers. This regimental flag displayed the British union in the canton, a heraldic badge in the center, and in each of three corners, a prancing white horse. William Washington's dragoons carried the only American flag known to have been in the battle—a banner of rose-colored damask that had been cut from the back of a chair.

From New York, George Washington rapidly marched his army south to Virginia accompanied by a large French force. At Yorktown, Pvt. Joseph Martin later remembered, when the trenches were dug and the French and American batteries were in place, the signal to begin the bombardment was the raising of the American flag. Martin wrote: *(Continued on page 66)*

Seeking words "so plain and firm as to command . . . assent," Thomas Jefferson drafted the Declaration of Independence, with "judgments and amendments" from Ben Franklin and John Adams (opposite).

At Monmouth in June 1778, Mary Hays (above) earned the nickname "Molly Pitcher" by carrying water to thirsty troops. According to legend, when her husband fell in battle, she seized the rammer and continued to fire his cannon. Though the artist included the Stars and Stripes, there is no evidence of its presence on the battlefield.

Crisp ranks of American and French soldiers dignify the occasion as 8,000 British troops lay down their arms at Yorktown on October 19, 1781, effectively ending the Revolutionary War. The British commander, Lord Cornwallis, chose not to surrender in person, sending his sword with a deputy. General Washington promptly designated his own deputy, Gen. Benjamin Lincoln, riding the white charger, to receive it.

In John Trumbull's painting, the Americans assemble under a flag with 12 stars squarely framing the 13th. Another depiction of the scene shows an American banner whose "new constellation" of stars appears to have been randomly sprinkled. The vague wording of the flag resolution passed by Congress in 1777 opened the door to much artistic license. But it is likely that only regimental flags flew at Yorktown; official records indicate that in spite of frequent requests for national colors, George Washington did not receive any flags until March 1783.

Benjamin Franklin: America's Premier Diplomat

When the colony of Pennsylvania wanted to present its views to England's government in 1757, their well-rounded delegation included an inventor, a postmaster, a printer, a civic leader, a writer, a scientist, and a statesman—in short, they sent Benjamin Franklin. Well-known on both sides of the Atlantic for his experiments with electricity, he had owned his own print shop, published a newspaper, written *Poor Richard's Almanack,* invented the lightning rod, helped establish the first free library in Philadelphia, and been elected to the Pennsylvania Assembly. His elevation to Britain's Royal Society gave him entrée in England, and his zest for living won him many friends.

Enjoying life in London, Franklin often affirmed the desirability of union between the mother country and America, even while trying to persuade the British government to limit the power of proprietors in the Colonies. As England pursued a course of heavy-handed force and taxation, Franklin, still personally conciliatory, defended Ameri-

can rights with a series of political essays and satires. In January 1774, in what one historian termed "a fatal error," the Privy Council denounced and insulted Franklin (opposite) for actions taken by Boston patriots without his knowledge. By the time Franklin sailed for home, he had become a firm supporter of independence and a formidable enemy of Britain.

In 1776 the 70-year-old revolutionary traveled to Canada to seek allies, served in the Continental Congress, helped write the Declaration of Independence, and sailed to Europe as America's minister to France. Fascinated as much by his plain clothes and fur cap as by his wit and wisdom, French ladies cooed over "Papa Franklin" (left).

Assisted by Arthur Lee and Silas Deane, Franklin worked hard to win critical aid from the French. He negotiated loans and supplies, gathered intelligence, hired European officers, including the brilliant Baron von Steuben, to help the American army, and cultivated influential officials. He also outfitted a "little American squadron"

so John Paul Jones could raid British shipping. Jones named his flagship the *Bonhomme Richard* in Franklin's honor.

Encouraged by the American victory at Saratoga, the French decided to align themselves openly with America. At the signing of the alliance, the normally soberly-dressed Franklin dazzled observers with a richly colored coat—the same one he had worn when rebuked by the Privy Council. Franklin was also on hand in September 1783 to sign the peace treaty with the British, saying "We are now Friends with England and with all Mankind."

Amid clouds of gun smoke, British redcoats launch an invasion of the city of Washington on August 24, 1814. Telescoping geography, a period English print shows the Brit- ish facing Americans in well-built fortifications at the city's perimeter. In fact, the main defense of the capi- tal occurred at Bladensburg, Mary- land, seven miles to the north. Despite the support of heavy naval cannon, hauled overland from Washington and manned by disci- plined American sailors, the inexpe- rienced militia was quickly routed

by 4,500 seasoned British soldiers. The redcoats then marched unopposed to the city, where they looted and burned the Capitol, the President's Mansion, and other gov- ernment buildings. This second war between the United States and Britain flared in June 1812 over English violations of American neutrality on the high seas. Through 30 months of fighting on land and sea, neither side could hold an advantage, though the destruction of Washington rallied the Americans to a string of victories.

The Flag in War and Diplomacy   **65**

Scaling the ramparts of Chapultepec Castle, the key to Mexico City, U. S. Army troops overwhelm Mexican defenders in hand-to-hand fighting (opposite). Seeing the Stars and Stripes flying over the stone fortress, ancient site of the Aztec Halls of Montezuma, the defeated Mexican commander, Gen. Santa Anna, said, "I think God himself is a Yankee."

The Mexican War began with a boundary dispute in the spring of 1846, after the United States annexed Texas. Outgunned and outfought, Mexico did not win a single battle in the two-year war. By the Treaty of Guadalupe Hidalgo, ratified March 10, 1848, the United States won the disputed part of Texas plus New Mexico and California; in return, Mexico was paid $15 million.

The official American flag was carried into battle by the U. S. Army for the first time in the Mexican War. The 27-star banner that probably accompanied the New Hampshire volunteers (above) in 1846 would have been two stars out of date by the end of the war.

"I felt a secret pride swell my heart when I saw the 'star-spangled banner' waving majestically . . . ; it appeared like an omen of success."

Under siege by sea and by land, Cornwallis surrendered on October 19, 1781. Washington, in retaliation for an earlier British insult to American troops at Charleston, denied his enemy the honors of war. Cornwallis's soldiers gave up their arms and marched out with drums beating dispiritedly and colors cased.

In Paris, Benjamin Franklin, John Jay, John Adams, and Henry Laurens negotiated peace with the British. Britain recognized the independence of the new nation and its boundaries—from the Atlantic to the Mississippi River, from Canada to Florida. But the United States did not begin life free of the British. Soon Great Britain and France were again at war, and both harassed American shipping. The British impressment of American seamen was especially insulting. In addition, the British still stirred up Indian warfare on the American side of the Canadian border.

In June 1812, Congress voted to declare war. At first, American land offenses failed, but at sea American privateers easily moved in and out of harbors and seized British merchant ships by the hundred. Commodore Oliver Hazard Perry won an American naval victory on Lake Erie in

Gunboat Diplomacy: Perry Opens Trade With Japan

Combining showmanship with a show of force, Commodore Matthew Perry (right) inveigled his way into Japan in July 1853, hoping to gain a treaty that would draw that isolated country into "the family of civilized nations." Anchoring in Tokyo Bay, his squadron of steam frigates and sailing vessels both frightened and fascinated the Japanese, who snapped up hastily printed woodcuts of the "black ships of evil mien" (below). Perry's tactic of refusing to be seen by any but the highest Japanese officials soon won him the title of "His High and Mighty Mysteriousness." When the

Emperor's emissary arrived, Perry came ashore with all possible pomp, only partly conveyed by the Japanese printmakers (opposite, bottom left). Flanked by two tall, black bodyguards, he was accompanied by an escort of sailors and marines and a band playing "Hail, Columbia." He delivered a letter from President Millard Fillmore and promised to return in the spring for a reply.

In March 1854 the Japanese agreed to America's principal demands, promising to assist shipwrecked sailors, to open two harbors to American ships, and to receive an American consul. The pact was sealed with an exchange of hundreds of official presents (opposite, top). Among the Japanese offerings were rolls of silk, jars of soy sauce, and assorted seashells. Perry's gifts to the emperor included a miniature steam engine with track, two telegraph sets, and Audubon's *Birds of North America* in nine volumes.

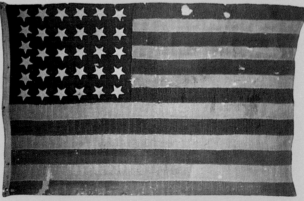

Americans saluted Perry's memory in 1945 by flying the commodore's own flag (above) aboard the U.S.S. *Missouri* when Japan surrendered to the United States, ending World War II.

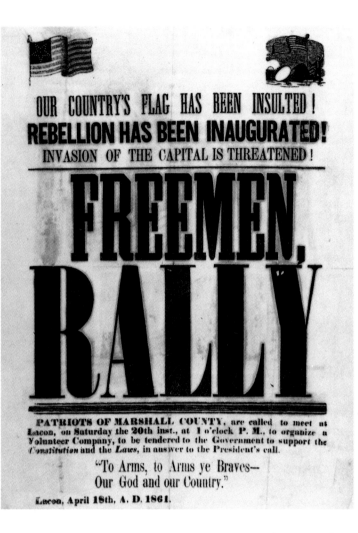

OUR COUNTRY'S FLAG HAS BEEN INSULTED !
REBELLION HAS BEEN INAUGURATED!
INVASION OF THE CAPITAL IS THREATENED !

FREEMEN, RALLY

PATRIOTS OF MARSHALL COUNTY, are called to meet at Lacon, on Saturday the 20th inst., at 1 o'clock P. M., to organize a Volunteer Company, to be tendered to the Government to support the *Constitution* and the *Laws*, in answer to the President's call.

"To Arms, to Arms ye Braves—
Our God and our Country."

Lacon, April 18th, A. D. 1861.

News of the Union surrender at Fort Sumter galvanized both North and South. Posters such as this one urged men to rally to the flag; in New York, more than 100,000 people gathered under the tattered banner salvaged from Fort Sumter to demand vengeance. In Charleston, reported a London paper, men strutted through the streets, "the battle blood running through their veins." Everywhere, men rushed to enlist in their army of choice—no doubt encouraged by a song popular with their womenfolk: "I Am Bound to Be a Soldier's Wife or Die an Old Maid."

September 1813, as did Commodore Thomas Macdonough on Lake Champlain a year later.

Meanwhile, a British army burned Washington, D. C., but failed to capture Baltimore. Thousands of British troops were sent to attack New Orleans, the key to control of the Mississippi Valley. Andrew Jackson, with a force of mostly Kentucky and Tennessee militiamen, faced the British on a narrow strip of land between the Mississippi and a wilderness of cypress swamps. The battle lasted half an hour. British casualties numbered more than 2,000; the Americans', only 70. Neither side had received word that a treaty to end the War of 1812 had been signed in Belgium two weeks earlier.

Sectionalism threatened the United States long before South Carolina seceded from the Union in 1860, widening the rift that led to the Civil War. Disputes between the southern states and the federal government had festered over the spread of slavery into the western territories and over trade tariffs, which were thought by the South to favor northern industries. In 1830, South Carolina Senator Robert Hayne launched an attack on New England, defending the view that state legislatures could nullify federal law. To the great orator Daniel Webster, Senator from Massachusetts, such doctrine endangered the Union itself. Webster, invoking the American flag, rose to the challenge: "When my eyes shall be turned to behold for the last time the sun in heaven . . . [let them see] the gorgeous ensign of the republic, now known and honored throughout the earth, still full high advanced, not a stripe erased or polluted, nor a single star obscured, bearing for its motto . . . Liberty and Union, now and forever, one and inseparable!"

For four horrible years it was not to be.

When the news of Abraham Lincoln's 1860 election to the Presidency reached Savannah, Georgia, secessionists rallied under a banner from the past. It showed a coiled rattler and proclaimed "Southern Rights" and "Don't Tread on Me." Following South Carolina's lead, Mississippi, Florida, Alabama, Georgia, and Louisiana left the Union and, in February 1861, established the Confederate States of America. Texas soon joined them. Within the year Virginia, Arkansas, North Carolina, and Tennessee seceded as well.

On April 12, 1861, South Carolina guns fired on Union troops at Fort Sumter in Charleston Harbor. Inside the fort, Maj. Robert Anderson and his 75 men did their best to repel a 34-hour bombardment. On the morning of April 13, Anderson surrendered to the Confederate commander, Brig. Gen. Pierre Beauregard, once Anderson's student at West Point. Over the fort flew a 33-star United States flag. Beauregard gave the departing Anderson permission to fire a 100-gun salute to "the flag which you have upheld so long and with so much fortitude." Partway through the salute, explosions killed one gunner and wounded five others, one fatally. These were the Civil War's first casualties.

Anderson and his men carried away their flag *(Continued on page 76)*

Flags, striped and barred, figured prominently in the songs of the Civil War. Supporters of Jefferson Davis sang this touching "farewell" to the Stars and Stripes at his inauguration as President of the Confederacy.

Overleaf: Commanding the heights, Union artillerymen prepared for battle at Chancellorsville, Virginia, in May 1863, where Gen. Robert E. Lee's bold tactics scored a victory for the South. States' rights and the abolition of slavery, the issues that set brother against brother, cost the nation dearly; four years of fighting brought casualties numbering more than a million, including 620,000 dead.

Flags of the Civil War

Struggling to distinguish itself from the United States, the Confederacy found successful flag design elusive. For their first, unofficial flag, Southerners borrowed elements of the United States banner, to which they considered themselves to have a legitimate claim. The new flag featured a circle of stars, one for each Confederate state, in a canton of blue, with wide red and white stripes. Almost immediately, at Bull Run in July 1861, the Rebels discovered that in the confusion of battle their Stars and Bars (opposite, top) were almost indistinguishable from the Stars and Stripes. Military leaders then adopted as their battle flag the familiar Southern Cross, a striking design of stars on a blue saltire,

or X-shape, against a red square (opposite, middle). The Confederate Congress decided to create an official flag by using the battle flag, recognized throughout the South, as the canton on a background of white, but this also proved unsatisfactory. The huge field, when hanging limp, could be easily mistaken for a flag of surrender. A third design (opposite, bottom), which corrected this defect by adding a red vertical stripe, was selected too late in the life of the Confederacy to make any appearance in public.

Whatever the flag, the job of flag-bearer was dangerous. In a fight, each side attempted to capture or destroy the enemy's colors. Sgt. William Smith (opposite, right) led troops in a charge against a Union position at Petersburg in 1864. Afterward, unhurt himself, he counted 75 bullet holes in his flag. Less lucky was Sgt. William Carney (opposite, left), of the 54th Massachusetts Infantry, the North's first black regiment. In an attack on Fort Wagner near Charleston, he seized the flag from a fallen comrade and carried it to the ramparts. When the Union assault failed, Carney retired the colors in good order. He was shot four times; his courage under fire won him the Medal of Honor.

Both sides drew comfort and inspiration from the sight of their respective banners flying above the fray. Parties of women, like this group in Philadelphia (opposite, right), met to sew colors for presentation to new regiments. Many of these flags, faded and torn, survived the war and were carefully saved, treasured reminders of comrades and times gone but not forgotten.

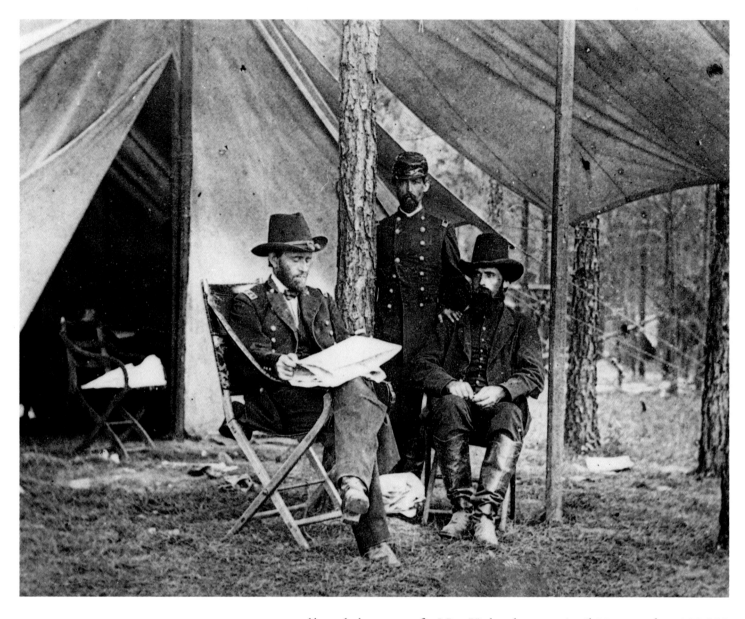

and boarded a steamer for New York, where, on April 20, more than 100,000 people rallied around the banner, its field of stripes torn by shot.

The day after the evacuation of Fort Sumter, a British war correspondent, William Howard Russell, traveled through North Carolina, which had not yet seceded from the Union. Russell saw the Confederate flag flying in towns and villages and heard cheers for "southern rights" and for the Confederacy's President Jefferson Davis. Of the flags, with seven stars in a circle and broad bars, two red and one white, Russell observed, "These pieces of bunting seem to twine themselves through heart and brain."

The Confederate flag evolved; stars were added as the number of rebelling states increased to 11. Two more stars followed in recognition of southern sympathizers in Kentucky and Missouri. The Stars and Bars

Officers and gentlemen, Generals Ulysses S. Grant and Robert E. Lee brought an end to the Civil War and gave the nation enduring models of military character. Described as "audacity personified" in battle, the silver-haired Lee (shown seated, this page) surrendered with grace at Appomattox and quietly encouraged his men to go home and "make as good citizens as you have soldiers." Grant (with map, opposite), as magnanimous in victory as he was relentless in war, allowed generous terms. Admonishing his own men against unseemly exultation, Grant said simply, "The war is over. The Rebels are our countrymen again."

proved to be so similar in appearance to the Stars and Stripes, unless waving broadly, that it led to disastrous confusion at the First Battle of Bull Run, on July 21, 1861; soldiers hardly knew which standard to follow amid the smoke from cannon and musket fire.

At Bull Run, Confederate armies triumphed. Early in 1862, Lincoln ordered all Union forces to advance against the Confederacy by land and by sea. Gen. George B. McClellan prepared his Army of the Potomac and began to move, but with many delays and miscalculations. As Robert E. Lee took command of the Confederate Army of Northern Virginia, McClellan stood within sight of Richmond, then—wrongly assuming that he was outnumbered—abandoned the campaign and retreated. In the autumn of 1862, after a second engagement at Bull Run had ended

Charged with driving Indians off the Great Plains and onto reservations, Lt. Col. George A. Custer (right) rashly attacked a large band of Cheyenne and Sioux camped by the Little Bighorn River in June 1876.

"Like bees swarming," some 2,000 Indians fell on Custer and his men and annihilated them in what is now widely known as "Custer's Last Stand." Spiritual and political leader Sitting Bull (left), stayed in camp

during the battle. He had a vision the week before that a great victory would be delivered to his people.

In this drawing of the fight, the Sioux chief Red Cloud casually rendered the soldiers' American flags upside down, but painstakingly depicted the murder and mutilation inflicted by the Indians in their last great victory against their enemy, the land-grabbing white man.

YOUR
COUNTRY
CALLS YOU

R·M·WRIG '98

With the explosion of an American battleship in Havana harbor (opposite), "Remember the Maine!" became the rallying cry of the Spanish-American War of 1898. Already sympathetic to Cuban patriots fighting against their Spanish oppressors, and egged on by the media, including this magazine cover (above), America declared war on Spain. Described afterward as "a splendid little war," the fighting lasted only ten weeks.

indecisively, Lee invaded the North. On September 15 half of his men, under Gen. Thomas J. "Stonewall" Jackson, captured Harpers Ferry, West Virginia.

On September 17, near the town of Sharpsburg, Maryland, Lee occupied a ridge between the Potomac River and Antietam Creek. McClellan assaulted the Confederates again and again. As the battle raged, Lee and a lieutenant named Ramsay watched troops advancing under clouds of smoke. Through his telescope, Ramsay identified them by their United States flag. Another column approached from the right. Ramsay focused again. His report that the color-bearers carried the Virginia and Confederate flags told Lee that reinforcements had arrived from Harpers Ferry.

In either army, color-bearers made splendid targets. Sometimes one after another met death as each took the flagstaff from his fallen comrade. Color-bearers found many ways to protect their flags from capture. One burned his flag in a campfire. Another wrapped the flag around a stone and sank it in the river. When capture or surrender seemed imminent, men sometimes shared the life-giving symbolism by cutting up the banners and distributing the small pieces among the soldiers.

Not only soldiers figured in such tales. In Nashville, Tennessee, a retired sea captain named William Driver—loyal to the Union—feared for the safety of the American flag he had once flown at sea, and almost 40 years before named "Old Glory." When Tennessee seceded from the Union, Captain Driver hid the flag inside a bed cover. Early in 1862, Union troops marched into Nashville after a successful campaign for control of the Tennessee and Cumberland Rivers. In the company of a Union officer, Driver retrieved his flag and raised it above the state capitol. His

deed, his praise of Old Glory, and subsequent publicity gave the nation another name for its flag.

The high tide of the Confederacy came in late 1862 and the spring of 1863 when, in Virginia, Lee inflicted a disastrous defeat on the forces of Maj. Gen. Ambrose Burnside at Fredericksburg and humiliated Burnside's successor, "Fighting Joe" Hooker, at Chancellorsville. Again Lee turned north and met the army of Gen. George G. Meade at Gettysburg, in southern Pennsylvania, but had to retreat again into Virginia. The Union victory at Gettysburg marked the beginning of the end for the Confederate military.

By the summer of 1863, Federal forces had taken New Orleans,

Memphis, and Vicksburg, thereby gaining control of the Mississippi River and severing Arkansas, Louisiana, and Texas from the rest of the Confederacy. Later that year, fighting seesawed across Tennessee and Georgia. In March 1864, Lincoln named a new commander of the Union Army—Ulysses S. Grant, soon to be known as "Unconditional Surrender Grant." Under Grant, Gen. William Tecumseh Sherman attacked the Confederacy from the west. He took Atlanta on September 2, and set out to crush the will of southern civilians. In November he began his march to the sea, cutting a 60-mile-wide swath of ruin, provisioning his army off the land and destroying what he could not use. Four days before Christmas 1864, Sherman reached his goal. On the 22nd he telegraphed Lincoln: "I beg to present you as a Christmas gift the city of Savannah . . . ."

In the meantime, Grant pursued Lee's army in Virginia. Early in April 1865, Grant forced the Confederates to evacuate their capital, Rich-

Patriotic fervor struck Americans again in April 1917, when Congress declared war on Germany and pushed the United States into global conflict. Flags, bunting, and posters decked homes, schools, shops, and churches in such profusion that it seemed as if victory had already been won. Enthusiasm stopped short of enlistment, however; the government had to resort to conscription, eventually drafting 2.8 million men into the Army.

Blacks, turned away as volunteers, made their way into the Army through the Selective Service Act. These black recruits being outfitted at Fort Meade, Maryland (left), were assigned to segregated units. The all-black 369th Infantry, dubbed the "Hell Fighters" by the Germans, received the French Croix de Guerre for exceptional gallantry in action.

mond. Lee retreated, his men exhausted and starving. Near the village of Appomattox Court House, the Federals captured Lee's desperately needed supply trains and cut off his line of march. Lee knew that he must surrender.

On April 9, Palm Sunday, the two generals met and agreed to terms. When the Confederates broke camp, Maj. Gen. Joshua Chamberlain watched them head toward him in "gray columns of march. On they come, with the old swinging route step and swaying battle-flags. In the van, the proud Confederate ensign." Chamberlain remembered that from the Union troops came "not a sound of trumpet . . . not a cheer . . . but an awed stillness rather, and breath-holding, as if it were the passing of the dead." The two armies saluted each other.

On April 14, now-retired Maj. Gen. Robert Anderson stood within the ruins of Fort Sumter, where, four *(Continued on page 90)*

The Flag in Patriotic Propaganda

The fine art of persuasion flourishes in wartime. During World War I, the Stars and Stripes appeared thousands of times in a wide variety of dramatic posters and paintings. To spur enlistments, the United States government mobilized the stern, guilt-inducing visage of Uncle Sam (below). Always attired in red, white, and blue, Uncle Sam's best-known incarnation was drawn by illustrator James Montgomery Flagg, who modeled Sam on himself. Flagg's Uncle Sam often appeared on magazine covers accompanied by Miss Liberty, a charming young woman also dressed in stars and stripes.

In pieces such as "No Longer Friends" (right), artists took note of, and promoted, anti-German sentiment,

NO LONGER FRIENDS

I WANT YOU
FOR U.S. ARMY
NEAREST RECRUITING STATION

which at times was taken to extremes. In some places, public performance of music by German composers was banned. Libraries burned German books. Names with German associations were changed: Hamburger became "Salisbury steak"; sauerkraut was renamed "liberty cabbage." Dachshunds were called "liberty pups."

Patriotic signs struck every possible emotional chord. Entreaties to buy Liberty bonds, many executed by the leading illustrators of the day, typically appealed to loyalty by portraying a soldier as a hero charging with, or wrapped in, the Stars and Stripes. Recruitment posters were designed to zing the conscience; a stalwart sailor urging enlistment challenged, "Don't read American history, MAKE IT!" Depictions of the enemy as the epitome of evil

War Gardens Victorious

Every War Garden a Peace Plant—
NATIONAL WAR GARDEN COMMISSION
— Charles Lathrop Pack, President   WASHINGTON, D.C.

OVER THE TOP FOR YOU

Buy U.S. Gov't Bonds
THIRD LIBERTY LOAN

and the destroyer of families and homes heightened fears.

Pictorial placards also encouraged families to make sacrifices at home: Heatless Mondays and meatless Tuesdays meant more resources for soldiers. Americans who trooped to their backyards to grow their own vegetables in "liberty gardens" (above, right) made a substantial contribution to the war effort. And so did the artists who mobilized along with everyone else. They gave us enduring images of war—and of ourselves.

U·S·A BONDS

Third
Liberty Loan
Campaign
BOY SCOUTS
OF AMERICA

WEAPONS FOR LIBERTY

Flag-draped coffins, row upon row, await memorial rites at a depot somewhere in Europe before final burial. During World War I, as in the Civil War, soldiers' remains often received quick but temporary burial after battle. After the war ended in 1918, they were disinterred and reburied in military cemeteries in Europe or shipped home at family request.

U.S. Leadership in the Forum of Nations

Those who survived the devastation of World War I sought two things: a lasting peace and a better way to settle differences. President Woodrow Wilson brought to the Paris Peace Conference a plan to satisfy these two longings. His program, called the Fourteen Points, included new borders for Europe, addressed issues such as free trade and open seas, and dearest to Wilson's heart, proposed an organization of nations to promote peace.

The plan was admired by many but accepted by few. Other delegates had their own ideas. To accommodate them, the three most important leaders (right)—Britain's David Lloyd George, France's Georges Clemenceau, and President Wilson—"crawled around on their knees on large maps spread on the floor, redrawing the boundaries of the nations of Europe." The final Treaty of Versailles imposed harsh conditions on Germany, making another conflict almost inevitable. One American general predicted, "It will have to be done all over again."

The delegates did endorse the League of Nations, on which rested Wilson's hopes for peace. But sadly, the Democratic President was not able to persuade the Republican Congress at home to sign the treaty or join the League. In spite of this, 48 other countries joined in 1920, and Woodrow Wilson received the Nobel Peace Prize.

From its home in Geneva (opposite, top), the League managed to halt slave trade and regulate air traffic. However, its charter stipulated that a vote must be unanimous to carry; thus the League as a whole could not enforce action against a single member. When Germany again became the aggressor in Europe, the League was powerless.

In the early days of World War II, two great leaders, Winston Churchill and Franklin Roosevelt, drafted the Atlantic Charter, a statement of war aims. The 26 allies who

signed it, calling themselves the "United Nations," became the basis for a new international peacekeeping organization. Even before the war ended, delegates met to work out details of the United Nations, which would be headquartered in New York (opposite, bottom). This time, they corrected the problems that plagued the League of Nations—the vote, the veto, the funding—and they included the power to send UN troops to intervene when necessary. Present at its creation, President Harry S. Truman warned, "If we fail to use it, we shall betray all those who have died in order that we might meet here in freedom and safety to create it."

Jolted from sleep, a pajama-clad man watches Japanese planes bomb Pearl Harbor on December 7, 1941. The surprise attack, at 7:55 on a Sunday morning, devastated the U. S. naval base, home of the Pacific fleet. Within two hours, waves of Japanese aircraft sank three battleships, including the U.S.S. West Virginia (opposite). They also damaged another 15 ships, destroyed airfields, and disabled some 200 planes on the ground. Sailors managed to rescue some of their comrades from burning oil slicks, but more than 2,400 American soldiers, sailors, and marines were killed. As survivors mourned their dead with flags and flowers (opposite, bottom), President Roosevelt condemned the attack as "unprovoked and dastardly," and Congress declared war on Japan. Though seriously crippled in the Pacific, Americans entered the world war united and determined on an all-out effort.

years earlier, he had met defeat. Now he raised over Charleston Harbor the same tattered Stars and Stripes that he had once carried away.

Within hours Abraham Lincoln died of a gunshot wound to the head, assassinated by southern sympathizer John Wilkes Booth, who held him responsible for the war. In the North, flags sank to half staff for more than a month as people mourned.

On May 23 and 24, General Grant and the new President, Andrew Johnson, reviewed victorious troops marching past the White House. Bands played the "Star-Spangled Banner." Flag-waving crowds cheered. The celebration took place under a 35-star flag—during the war, Kansas and West Virginia had joined the Union. Through all the years of battle, Lincoln had refused to allow the removal of stars representing the rebellious states. The American flag, even in a Union asunder, always held the promise of a Union restored.

By the end of the 19th century, America's expansionist spirit looked outward. When the battleship *Maine* exploded in the harbor of Havana, Cuba, on February 15, 1898, killing 260 men, events that followed made an imperial power of a ready and willing United States. *(Continued on page 96)*

Overleaf: Wading into a hail of German machine-gun fire, Allied troops invade France on D-Day, June 6, 1944. Disgorged from box-like landing craft along a 60-mile strip of coastline in Normandy, the soldiers established beachheads and cleared the way for the largest amphibious invasion in history. At the section dubbed Omaha Beach, resistance was fierce; the Americans "barely held on by their eyelids." Fifteen Allied divisions poured onto the beaches over the next five days to begin the liberation of Europe.

Rosie the Riveter and the Home Front

When American men donned uniforms and went to war, American women put on slacks and went to work. As World War II pulled 15 million men from the labor force, managers turned to women reluctantly, believing them too frail to handle machinery. Women quickly proved them wrong, soon filling many jobs traditionally held by men: welder, truck driver, mail carrier. "Rosie the Riveter," a fictional character clad in overalls and holding a rivet gun, became a popular symbol. Employment ads read, "If you can make a cake, then you can put powder in a shell casing." By 1944, females held 40 percent of the jobs in aircraft assembly plants (above, right) and 12 percent of those in shipyards. A

sign of the times (below, left) tacitly acknowledged the composition of the new work force; typical munitions makers (below, right) display a shell addressed "To Hitler from Lone Star Girls."

Folks at home supported the war effort in every possible way: growing vegetables; knitting socks; doing without butter, toys, shoes, gas. A giant cash register in New York City (opposite) tallied sales as Americans bought war bonds. Sacrifice, the primary weapon of the home front, helped tip the balance on the battlefield.

Every bomb-load counts ..MAKE 'EM RIGHT!

The Big Three—Allied leaders Winston Churchill, Franklin Roosevelt, and Joseph Stalin—met at Yalta in the Crimea in February 1945 (right) to shape the new Europe that would come into being at the end of the war. The agreement Churchill and Roosevelt forged with Stalin, which depended on good faith, created the framework for the Cold War even before World War II had ended.

The mushroom cloud of the atomic bomb dropped on Nagasaki (opposite) brought an end to the war with Japan in August 1945—and further skewed the balance of power. Now the threat of nuclear war, as well as Russian aggression, overshadowed the long-awaited peace.

Cuba was in rebellion against Spanish rule. American sympathies, inflamed by a jingoistic press, lay with the rebels. Diplomatic negotiations secured a Spanish promise of autonomy for the island. Even so, after riots in Cuba in January 1898, President McKinley ordered the *Maine* to Havana, ostensibly to protect American citizens and property. After the explosion, Theodore Roosevelt declared, "The *Maine* was sunk by an act of dirty treachery on the part of the Spaniards," although he lacked evidence to support his conclusion. Even today, no one knows why the ship blew up, but the United States rang with the cry "Remember the *Maine !*" In April, Congress declared war against Spain.

By the end of June, U. S. Army troops landed in Cuba to attack Santiago. With them was Col. Leonard Wood's volunteer cavalry regiment, best known as the Rough Riders, and noted for its second-in-command, Lt. Col. Theodore Roosevelt. On foot, the Rough Riders took part in a hard-fought but victorious contest remembered as the Battle of San Juan Hill.

A punishing land and naval bombardment of Santiago led to Spanish surrender on July 17. As a result of the war, the United States occupied Puerto Rico and Guam, annexed Hawaii, and, in the

Wearing snow-white camouflage, a U. S. Army infantry squad goes on patrol in Korea, where the Cold War turned hot in 1950. A microcosm of world politics, the Korean War began when Soviet-supported North Korea invaded South Korea, a U. S. ally. American troops went to war as part of a United Nations "police action." When Communist China buttressed North Korea, nuclear war threatened.

After three years of fighting, negotiations fixed the border between North and South near where it had been at the start of the war. Prisoners, like these North Koreans being marched across rice fields by U. S. Marines (opposite), were allowed to choose where they would live. The war ended inconclusively, with an armed truce rather than peace.

Philippines, quelled a rebellion against Americans. Theodore Roosevelt boasted, "We stand supreme in a continent, in a hemisphere."

In 1906, Roosevelt, then President, won the Nobel Peace Prize for his role as mediator in the settlement of the Russo-Japanese War, but his administration left a troublesome diplomatic legacy. Japan harbored resentment over some of the terms of the peace treaty. Roosevelt's high-handed encouragement of Panamanian rebels gave him the land he wanted for a canal across the Isthmus of Panama but worsened tensions between the United States and Latin America. "I took the canal zone," he said later, "and let Congress debate, and while the debate goes on, the canal does also."

The flag that flew with American forces in the Spanish-American War recorded the country's expansion as star after star had recognized the addition of new states. By 1898 there were 45. In 1907, Roosevelt sent the 45-star flag around the world with his Great White Fleet. Touted as a voyage of friendship, the fleet consisted of 16 battleships and was Roosevelt's demonstration—especially to the Japanese, about whom he was uneasy—of American naval strength. Japan, however, welcomed the fleet. Schoolchildren met it, singing the "Star-Spangled Banner" in English and waving little American flags.

The Panama Canal opened in August 1914, but war in Europe over-shadowed the long-awaited event and mocked the slogan of the Canal Zone, "The Land Divided, the World United."

Woodrow Wilson was President in June 1914 when, in the streets of far-off Sarajevo, a young Serbian nationalist killed the heir to the throne of Austria-Hungary. The assassination plunged the world into war.

Wilson, who admitted to being an idealist, once said, "That is the way I know I am an American." He saw the United States as a moral leader. The American flag, he said in 1914, "is the flag not only of America but of humanity." During the first years of the war, Wilson urged neutrality for the United States. He offered to mediate between the warring powers.

Even so, anti-German sentiment rose among Americans, especially after aggressive submarine warfare. On May 7, 1915, a German U-boat torpedoed the British liner *Lusitania*—which, like many ships in British waters, carried both passengers and arms for the Allies. The attack killed 1,198 people, including 128 Americans.

"Preparedness" became the cry of the day, both for Americans who favored neutrality and for those who advocated intervention. In 1916, Wilson, wearing a top hat and tailcoat, marched along New York streets in a flag-teeming "preparedness parade," and campaigned for a second term on the slogan "He kept us out of war."

In Europe, the fighting on Germany's eastern front had been indecisive. Early in March 1917, a revolution overthrew the autocracy of the Russian tsar, Nicholas II. The new Bolshevik government soon took Russia out of the war, a move that freed thousands of Germans to fight in France. In the same month, German submarines sank four American

President Dwight D. Eisenhower, hoping "to improve the outlook for peace," visited European and Eastern nations in December 1959. In Tehran, Iranians honored his arrival by flying Old Glory over an arch of friendship (opposite). Greeted everywhere by cheering, flower-throwing crowds, the President assured them of America's good will.

Interpreters look anxious as Vice President Richard Nixon argues the merits of free government with Russia's combative premier, Nikita Khrushchev. The "kitchen debate," which took place at an exhibit in Moscow featuring an American model home, typified U. S.-Soviet relations in the 1950s.

ships. Sorrowfully, Wilson asked Congress to declare war, affirming that "the world must be made safe for democracy."

In June the first of some two million American troops landed in France, paraded past cheering, flower-tossing Parisians, and announced, "Lafayette, we are here!" American participation in the fighting took place mostly in the last few months of the war, but U. S. forces played a critical role, and the Allies gained victories throughout the summer and fall of 1918. In the war's last major campaign, Gen. John J. Pershing led more than a million Americans, who fought alongside British and French soldiers on a wide front from the Meuse River to the ravines, hills, and thickets of the Argonne Forest. In the face of strong German resistance, the Allies persevered. In November the Germans collapsed and signed an armistice.

From the smoldering embers of the old war, a new conflagration soon would blaze. Although World War I had been, in Wilson's words, "the war to end all wars," in large measure it preordained World War II. Its legacy, said writer Edmund Stillman, was "a quality of despair, a chaos, and a drift toward political barbarism." Winston Churchill and many others objected to the treaties signed at the end of the war, which laid

Stars and stripes on bags of sorghum (above) identify aid from the United States. The relief supplies went to Somali nomads in refugee camps during the war with Ethiopia in 1977. Said one camp observer, "Everywhere I went, I saw food from America."

Peace Corps volunteers in Bolivia vaccinate a young girl against smallpox (opposite). The Peace Corps, launched by President John F. Kennedy, sends skilled volunteers to help developing nations with projects relating to small business, education, rural improvement, agriculture, and health. Since 1961, some 140,000 volunteers have served as ambassadors of American good will in more than 100 countries.

the foundation for Japanese expansionism in the 1930s. They fragmented several European countries and imposed harsh terms on a broken Germany. Widespread economic depression followed. A 29-year-old Austrian corporal named Adolph Hitler vowed revenge.

Early on the morning of December 7, 1941, U. S. Navy color guards raised the Stars and Stripes above the moored ships of the Pacific Fleet at Pearl Harbor, Hawaii. At five minutes before eight, the first Japanese bombs began to fall. The next day, Congress declared war on Japan. On December 11, Japan's Axis allies, Germany and Italy, retaliated by declaring war against the United States.

Germany had been at war with Britain and France since September 1939. During the 1930s, Hitler had become chancellor of Germany, anointed himself *der Führer,* and set upon his dark course. In 1939 he seized Austria, invaded Czechoslovakia and Poland, and in 1940 and 1941 marched into Denmark, Norway, Belgium, and the Netherlands. Italy and Germany carried the war to Yugoslavia, Greece, and North Africa. German planes began to bomb England. Hitler broke his nonaggression pact with the Soviet dictator Joseph Stalin and ordered a blockade of Leningrad that would last until 1944.

Roosevelt began to send arms, planes, and ships to Britain, and aid to the Soviet Union, which by the end of 1941, with the help of its old ally, winter, had driven the Germans back from Moscow. It was only a temporary respite. Hitler then ordered an attack against Stalingrad, where Germans and Russians fought hand-to-hand in streets, houses, and factories until the German commander surrendered on January 31, 1943. The Battle of Stalingrad and the final Allied victory in North Africa four months later

U. S. Marines at Khe Sanh dodge flying debris (right) as enemy shelling explodes an ammunition dump during the Vietnam War. American military involvement in the divided country of Vietnam began in 1955, when the U. S. sent a few advisers to help train the army of South Vietnam, threatened by aggressive Communists from the North. By 1969, 543,000 U. S. troops were engaged in the fight against North Vietnam. The South Vietnamese soldier above wore an American flag on his helmet to express solidarity with his allies. But the war proved unwinnable. The United States withdrew in 1973; South Vietnam fell to the Communists in 1975.

marked turning points in the war. The North African campaign, a triumph of strategy, demonstrated the diplomatic efforts of Gen. Dwight D. Eisenhower, the commander of the Allied forces, to forge cooperation among the Allied generals. From their African springboard, the Allies began to put pressure on Germany's weak ally, Italy. They liberated grateful Sicilians from German occupation, then began a two-pronged advance up the Italian peninsula.

In June 1944 a colossal war machine stood ready in southern England. Ships, planes, guns, bulldozers, half-tracks, tanks, and railroad cars by the thousand were assembled. Almost three million troops gathered.

A GI signals to a medical evacuation helicopter (opposite) as paratroopers help wounded comrades into a jungle clearing for rescue. The Vietnam conflict was the first war ever to be televised; the horrors of combat became standard fare on the evening news in the 1960s. Such scenes, coupled with a death toll that climbed to 57,939, caused many Americans to question U. S. involvement in Vietnam.

Thousands demonstrated against the war, the draft, and the government itself. Protesters, like this young man spiking military rifles with flowers (above), angered supporters of the war. While American men fought in Vietnam, Americans at home found themselves at war with each other.

General Eisenhower called it "a great human spring, coiled for the moment when its energy should be released and it would vault the English Channel in the greatest amphibious assault ever attempted."

At 6:30 on the morning of June 6, the first Allies hit the beaches of Normandy. A day of courageous, vicious, and sometimes chaotic fighting secured them a foothold, from which they pressed on. By August 25 they had liberated Paris. Other Allied troops made a second landing, in southern France, and advanced north to join their comrades who were pushing Hitler's troops back into their homeland.

Soviet armies marched into Germany from the east in January 1945. The next month, the Allies began to advance from the west. On April 12—the day that Franklin Roosevelt died in Warm Springs, Georgia—Eisenhower's troops reached the Elbe River. On April 25, Russians and Americans met near the Elbe town of Torgau. Picnic tables laden with wine and flowers stood beneath the trees, from which floated a banner brought from the east that read, "Our greetings to the brave troops of the First Amerikan Army."

Two weeks later, the people of the United States heard President Harry Truman announce the German surrender. "The flags of freedom," he said, "fly all over Europe."

The Flag in War and Diplomacy

At last the Allies could turn all their might against the other war. In the first six months after the attack on Pearl Harbor, the Japanese had invaded the Philippines, Guam, Wake Island, the Solomon Islands, and the Aleutians. Gen. Douglas MacArthur, having left the Philippine island of Corregidor with the vow "I shall return," was ordered to oversee the protection of Australia.

After the United States had stunned Japan with an air raid on Tokyo in April 1942, the Japanese determined to take the Midway Islands in the Pacific. In a battle that covered hundreds of square miles, carrier-launched bombers attacked and counterattacked. The American victory decisively punished the Japanese Navy and proved American carrier strength.

Far to the south of Midway, on August 7, 1942, United States Marines seized a Japanese airfield on Guadalcanal in the Solomon Islands. Then Japanese reinforcements swept in. For months, fierce land and naval battles raged until the Japanese evacuated in February 1943.

American forces continued their campaign to recapture Japan's Pacific bases. By January 1945, Americans had won control of Leyte Gulf in the Philippines and, two months later, recaptured Manila. On Corregidor, General MacArthur ordered: "Hoist the colors and let no enemy ever haul them down."

Now American bombers needed bases where they could refuel and resupply for air strikes on Japan. Two islands, Iwo Jima and Okinawa, became hard-won prizes as the Allies moved closer.

By midsummer 1945, American submarines, peering at Mount Fuji through periscopes, were blockading Japan, American planes were bombing Japanese cities, and American ships *(Continued on page 114)*

With a flag of flowers as a backdrop, a veteran weeps at the Vietnam Veterans Memorial in Washington, D.C., on Veterans Day, 1986 (opposite). The stark walls of polished black granite, chiseled with the names of every U. S. serviceman and woman killed or missing in the war, at first offended hawk and dove alike. But the moving tribute, which both honors the dead and emphasizes the terrible price of war, exercised a cathartic, healing power. In time, Americans bitterly divided over a lost cause began to face the difficult questions the war raised about the nature of patriotism and the country's role in foreign conflicts.

A striking tableau of flags and out-stretched hands marks the beginning of the end of the Cold War. At their first encounter in Geneva, in November 1985, Soviet Secretary General Mikhail Gorbachev and U. S. President Ronald Reagan "abandoned four decades of confron-tation" and began a warm friend-ship. At three more summit meetings, including one in Moscow where Russian children greeted Reagan with American flags (above), the two world leaders agreed to arms reduc-tions and began a new era of sur-prising and welcome cooperation.

Turning day into night, thick smoke billows from oil wells torched by Iraqis as they fled Kuwait in the 1991 Persian Gulf War. In a mighty display of military tactics, technology, and organization, a coalition of nations drove the Iraqis out of the tiny, oil-rich Arab country after five weeks of aerial bombing and one hundred hours of ground fighting. Of more than 540,000 U. S. troops engaged, only 144 were killed in action—little comfort to the sergeant (above) who just learned that his comrade had been killed by "friendly fire."

The Flag in War and Diplomacy

American forces arrive in Mogadishu, Somalia, in December 1992 as part of a United Nations-sponsored mission dubbed Operation Restore Hope. Some 17,000 U. S. Marine and Army troops joined 14,000 UN soldiers in Somalia to help distribute food shipments to rural areas, where nearly a third of the Somali population faced starvation because of the effects of clan warfare and drought.

were cruising the Japanese coast. Japan's navy was almost gone. Emperor Hirohito wanted peace, but his military leaders resisted. The United States faced a grim choice: invade Japan at a cost of hundreds of thousands of lives, or use the atomic bomb. On August 6 and 9, B-29s dropped the bomb on Hiroshima and Nagasaki. Japan surrendered on August 14.

From the mushroom clouds emerged a profoundly changed world. The United States, now the world's leading power in the nuclear age, locked horns with the Soviet Union in Cold War competition for the hearts and minds of smaller nations around the globe. In Korea, from 1950 to 1953, American and United Nations forces supporting South Korea battled against North Korea, which was backed by China and the Soviet Union.

In the same period, the United States began to subsidize France in its efforts to hold on to French colonial territory in Vietnam. But in 1954, Vietnamese Communists defeated the French, and the country was split into Communist North Vietnam and U. S.-supported South Vietnam. The next year, the South Vietnamese leader Ngo Dinh Diem repudiated the partition and named himself president of a Vietnamese republic. Soon Diem found himself at war with Communist-trained guerillas known as Vietcong.

The United States sent thousands of military "advisers" to South Vietnam. In August 1964, President Lyndon Johnson announced that North Vietnamese patrol boats had attacked two American destroyers in the Gulf of Tonkin, some 30 miles off the North Vietnamese coast. Congress granted Johnson the power to use armed force to "repel further aggres-

sion." Johnson ordered bombing raids over North Vietnam, and, in March 1965, sent in the first American combat troops. Two years later, more than half a million Americans were in Vietnam, along with some 60,000 troops from Australia, South Korea, and other anticommunist nations.

The Vietnam War was the longest in American history, and it solved nothing. In the early years of heavy fighting, both sides sustained major damage, but results were a draw. Gen. William Westmoreland aimed to wage a war of attrition, but the Communist forces replaced their losses.

Richard Nixon won the Presidency in 1968. In reaction to mounting antiwar sentiment, he began to withdraw American troops from Vietnam, but, at the same time, he built up the air war, secretly bombing Cambodia. Peace talks held in Paris produced no results until January 1973, when the United States signed an agreement accepting the presence of North Vietnamese troops in the south. In March the last U. S. combat troops left

The Flag in War and Diplomacy   115

The City of New York honors veterans of Operation Desert Storm with an old-fashioned ticker tape parade in June 1991. American troops fought in the Persian Gulf War as part of an unprecedented 28-nation coalition organized through the United Nations. Celebrating the triumph of international cooperation, President George Bush said, "Our spirits are as high as our flag—and our future is as bright as Liberty's torch."

Vietnam, but the war did not stop. Two years later, the North Vietnamese claimed victory.

The United Nations, born of hope near the end of World War II, saw its role changing over the decades as it faced new demands. In August 1990, when Iraqi troops invaded Kuwait and massed troops on the border of Saudi Arabia—both oil-rich Persian Gulf nations—the United Nations, with leadership from the United States, organized a coalition of 28 countries to pressure the Iraqis to leave Kuwait and abandon their plans for Saudi Arabia. The U. S. soon found itself fighting a dictatorship with which it had had a long and muddled relationship.

When economic sanctions against Iraq failed, coalition forces bombed Iraqi military and industrial targets. Then allied armies invaded Iraq and surrounded Iraqi forces in Kuwait in a hundred-hour ground war, forcing Iraq's withdrawal. The action sent a clear warning to would-be aggressors, but also left behind, for the United Nations and for the United States, many grave problems in the troubled Middle East.

Every major war fought by Americans has changed us in some way. The Revolutionary War gave us our nation. The Civil War tortured and redefined it. World War II built the bomb—and a prosperous postwar society. The Vietnam War tore us apart. But now the Cold War has ended and the world itself has changed, becoming once again a strange, new place in which to test the ideals of the Star-Spangled Banner.

The Flag in Exploration

The Flag in Exploration

ver the exploring entrepreneur, George Washington took time off in the spring of 1763 from his duties as delegate to Virginia's General Assembly to venture into the Dismal Swamp. With a group of partners—the Adventurers for Draining the Dismal Swamp—Washington hoped to harvest lumber and develop farmland. He measured off distances; observed that his horse negotiated the wet terrain with little difficulty; and judged the soil, by and large, to be dark, rich, and potentially "prodigeous fine."

Since the age of 16, when he had helped survey parts of the enormous land holdings of Thomas, Lord Fairfax, George Washington had been captivated by the American landscape. He came to dream of the Potomac River as an approach to the interior, to the Ohio country. As a young man in his twenties, Washington traveled on various missions across the Appalachian Mountains.

He led some 150 militiamen westward from Virginia in April 1754, carrying a map he had made the year before. He was under orders to build a fort where the Allegheny and Monongahela Rivers join to form the Ohio—a place known as the Forks of the Ohio. To reach their destination, Washington and his men followed Indian trails and hacked clearings through the wilderness, opening a road across the Alleghenies.

Soon after the Revolutionary War, Washington returned to his plans for a westward-expanding nation. In 1783, after exploring the headwaters of the Mohawk and the Susquehanna Rivers, he wrote to his friend the Marquis de Chastellux, "I shall not rest contented till I have explored the Western country, and transversed those lines, or great part of them, which have given bounds to a new empire."

The pioneering spirit that took man to the ends of the earth launched the effort to explore the frontier of space. Old Glory stands on the lunar surface beside astronaut Harrison H. Schmitt (opposite), the first geologist on the moon, who flew on Apollo 17 with Eugene A. Cernan and Ronald E. Evans in December 1972. From afar, almost a quarter of a million miles away, the home planet glows "small and blue and beautiful" in the blackness of space.

Legendary frontiersman Daniel Boone (above) rests during an outing in his beloved "Western" wilderness, its beauty exemplified by this sunrise at Pinnacle Overlook in Cumberland Gap National Historic Park (right). In the 1770s, Boone opened the Wilderness Road, following an old Indian trail through Cumberland Gap to Kentucky. There he established the permanent settlement of Boonesboro. For years the Wilderness Road served pioneers as the gateway to the West.

Muralist Barry Faulkner's tribute to Bostonian Capt. Robert Gray—the little-known discoverer of the mouth of the Columbia River—is mounted on a wall of the capitol rotunda in Salem, Oregon. The artist's modern conception depicts an imagined first encounter between the explorer and the local Chinook Indians, who offer pelts to the crew upon landfall in May 1792. As a symbol of peace, the crew proffers the flag. Gray made his first fur-trading voyage to the Pacific coast in 1790; his ship was one of many plying the Pacific in the late

18th century. On his return two years later, a southward course led him to the mouth of the river, which he named for his ship, the Columbia Rediviva, *shown anchored offshore.*

Sailing under the Stars and Stripes, Gray's expedition strengthened America's claim on the vast Oregon region, which extended from the Rockies to the Pacific, and north from

California—territory also claimed by Britain and by Spain. It fueled Thomas Jefferson's dream of establishing a river route to the Pacific and paved the way for the explorations of Lewis and Clark.

The Flag in Exploration

Charles Willson Peale portrayed explorers William Clark (left) and Meriwether Lewis (right) on their return from the Pacific. The artist installed the portraits in his unique museum of American history and science in Philadelphia's Independence Hall.

Four years apart in age, both explorers grew up in the Blue Ridge region of Virginia, Lewis near Charlottesville and Clark in nearby Caroline County. Legend wrongly links them as boyhood friends; in fact, they met later, in the mid-1790s, when Lewis joined a rifle company under Clark's command. All told, Lewis and Clark logged some 8,000 miles in their epic search for western trade routes and Indian trading partners.

In September 1784 he journeyed from Mount Vernon to visit his land west of the Appalachians and to investigate "the best communication between Eastern and Western waters." The next year he took the lead in founding the Patowmack Company, which improved the riverbed of the Potomac and built canals to skirt rapids and falls. From 1788 to 1830, in various stages of completion and efficiency, the waterway linked the thriving Potomac port of Georgetown with Cumberland, Maryland, and the Ohio country.

On April 30, 1789, Washington took the oath of office as the first President of the United States. The nation celebrated his Inauguration during an era characterized by historian William H. Goetzmann as "a worldwide commercial and imperial struggle in which exploration and emerging science played a vital part." One focus of this struggle in North America was the Pacific Northwest, with its rich fur trade and the old dream of a Northwest Passage. A Yankee fur trader and sea captain named Robert Gray discovered a northwest passage of sorts. And it was on Gray's flagship, *Columbia,* that the Stars and Stripes first sailed around the world.

In 1787, Gray left Boston, rounded Cape Horn, and made his way to Nootka Sound on the coast of British Columbia. There, in the spring and summer of 1789, he exchanged trade goods for sea otter pelts—highly prized in China. In December he sold the furs in Canton, took on a cargo

of tea, and in August 1790 sailed back into Boston Harbor to be greeted with a 13-gun salute.

A month later, Gray again left Boston bound for the Pacific Northwest. Here lay the mysterious "River of the West," which other explorers had only suspected—or missed completely. As Gray sailed along the coast, scouting for sheltered inlets and for Indians with furs, he observed a strong current pouring from a bay. A sandbar blocked the passage, but on May 11, 1792, the wind was favorable and the tide was right. Gray's log notes that his ship "ran in east-northeast between *(Continued on page 130)*

Among those who set out to visually capture the wild West, Karl Bodmer, a young Swiss artist, sketched this scene on the upper Missouri River in 1833. He later supervised the making of this hand-colored aquatint. Before their expedition upriver, Bodmer and his patron, German naturalist Prince Maximilian, met William Clark in St. Louis, where Clark introduced them to influential citizens and Indian delegations.

The Legacy of Lewis and Clark

Along with his blessings, President Jefferson gave Lewis and Clark specific instructions to record "with great pains and accuracy" everything they saw, then sent them on their westward way. They did not disappoint. Pooling their complementary professional skills—Lewis was the expedition scientist, and Clark the geographer, cartographer, and artist—the pair zealously observed and gathered facts, artifacts, and specimens during the course of their 28-month journey. They brought home a wealth of information—to Jefferson and to the nation.

Both men, along with at least five other expedition members, kept copious diaries. Clark carried this elkskin-bound field book (right, top) on his knee for making rough notes, later to be transcribed into his permanent journal—which also served as a sketchbook.

A talented draftsman, Clark frequently sketched the distinctive flora and fauna they encountered on the trail—in all, they recorded 122 new species and subspecies of mammals, reptiles, amphibians, fish, and birds, and almost 200 plants. Clark's much-praised sketch of a white salmon trout (right, bottom), which measured "2 feet 8 inches Long," took up a page of his March 1806 journal. Noting the Columbia River Indians' dependence on the trout and the salmon, Clark included a detailed description copied from Lewis's notes, which often served when time pressed. Of the many new birds they discovered, two species found near the Rockies in the summer of 1805 bear the explorers' names: Lewis's woodpecker (opposite, bottom left), brought home as a skin, and Clark's nutcracker (bottom right).

As they pushed west, Clark sketched many maps, using his own observations as well as those of Indians and other explorers. Probably his earliest, this 1804 chart (opposite, top) filled some gaps on the touted 1802 Arrowsmith map, Lewis and Clark's primary guide.

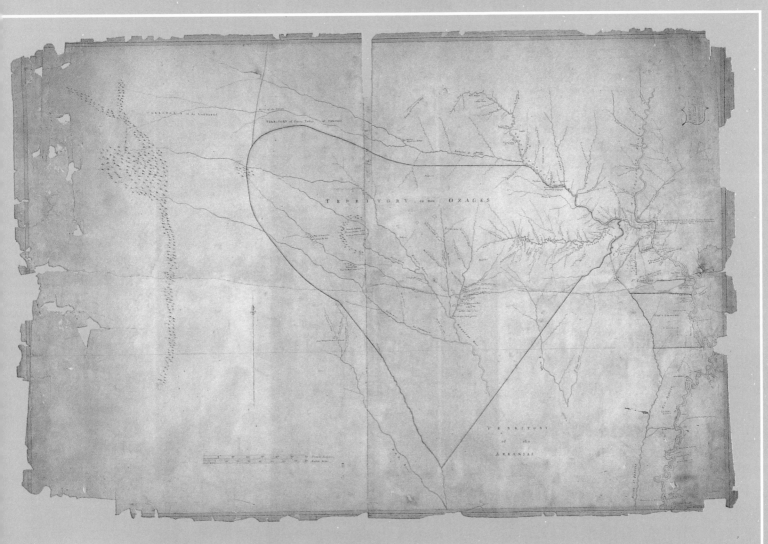

Edgar S. Paxson's mural in Montana's state capitol at Helena depicts Clark, Lewis, and French-Canadian interpreter Toussaint Charbonneau heeding Sacagawea as she points out recognizable land-marks near the Three Forks of the Missouri River, south of Great Falls, Montana. The party camped here before pressing on in their search for Sacagawea's people, the Shoshone, from whom Lewis and Clark would obtain horses for their arduous trek across the Bitterroot Range.

The only woman in the expedition, 17-year-old Sacagawea—"Bird Woman" in Hidatsa—had camped at the same spot five years earlier, when a marauding band of Hidatsa Indians took her off to the Dakotas. She was traded among warriors until Charbonneau, a trapper-trader living with the tribe, ac-quired her for his wife. With her infant son Jean Baptiste, Sacagawea accompanied the expedition from what is now North Dakota to the coast and back, her presence serving as a sign of peace, when necessary, in encounters with Indian nations.

Immortalized for a peak he saw but never climbed or named, Lt. Zebulon M. Pike (above), portrayed by Charles Willson Peale, may claim true fame as the first authorized American explorer to cross present-day Colorado. In 1805, Pike left St. Louis on his first expedition to find the headwaters of the Mississippi River—in Indian parlance "the Father of Waters"—which winds along for 2,348 miles. Unfortunately, Pike, with his poor sense of direction, misidentified the source, which is Lake Itasca—from the Latin for "true head"—near Bemidji, Minnesota (opposite). In 1806, however, he went on to map the territory west from St. Louis to Colorado, his greatest contribution.

the breakers, having from five to seven fathoms of water. When we were over the bar, we found this to be a large river of fresh water, up which we steered."

Even before the Louisiana Purchase in 1803, Thomas Jefferson had his eyes on the western regions and had determined to send an expedition to the Pacific. Jefferson's ambitions were as far-reaching as the continent itself. He instructed Meriwether Lewis and William Clark to explore and map a route along the Missouri River and its "communication with the waters of the Pacific Ocean." They were to take a census of Indians and make detailed reports on Indian life. Jefferson requested information on vegetation, animals, fossils, mineral resources, volcanoes, weather, topography, and the possibility of shipping furs and other goods via the Missouri.

He especially cautioned his Corps of Discovery about its relationship with Indians. The men were to be ambassadors—friendly and informative about the "peaceable & commercial dispositions of the U. S.," and they were to invite "influential chiefs" to visit the nation's capital.

When Lewis and Clark and some 47 men set out from St. Louis in May 1804, they carried in their baggage American flags of 3 sizes, each with 15 stars and 15 stripes. Occasionally in camp they flew the largest one. To chiefs, they presented flags of a size deemed appropriate to the recipient's rank. The Indians often raised these flags near their lodges. The explorers also bestowed medals, signed and dated certificates of friendship, and many other gifts including beads, paint, moccasin awls, pewter looking glasses, cocked hats, frock coats, and calico shirts.

In 1804, in their winter camp along the Missouri, Clark's journal recounts, they warned Mandan chiefs who had received medals and flags

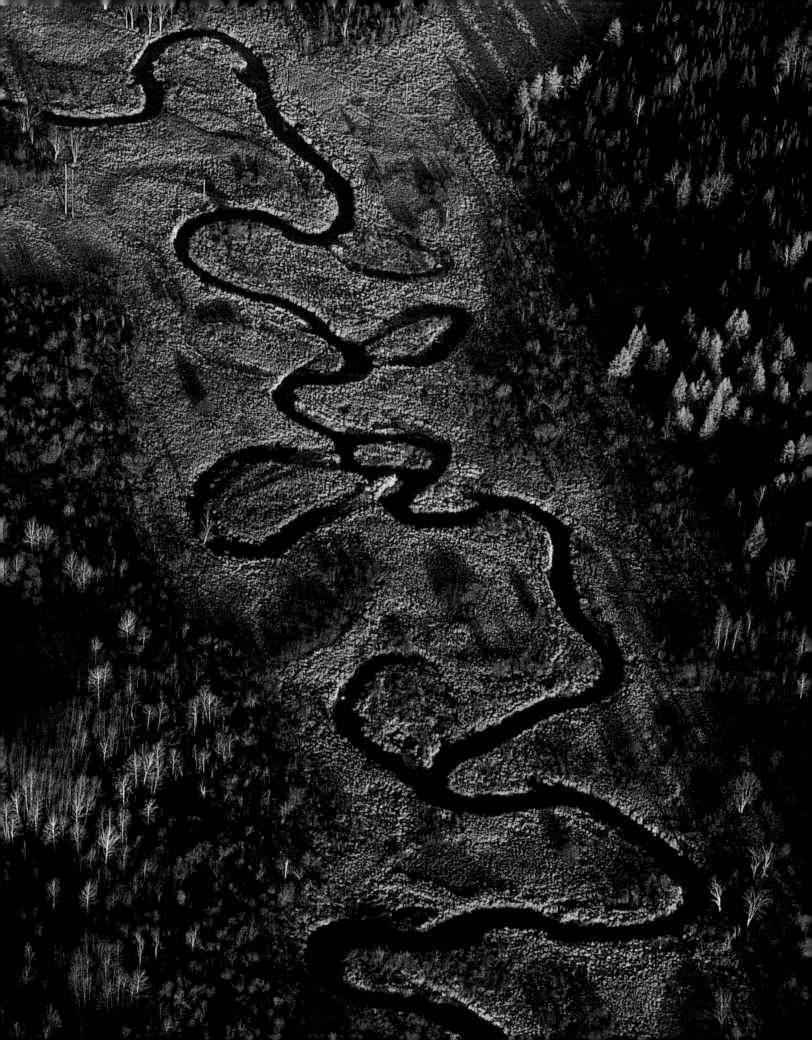

Rising 14,110 feet above sea level, the massif of Pikes Peak looms through Gateway Rocks, the present-day entrance to a 1,350-acre natural scenic park in Colorado Springs called Garden of the Gods. This passage represented a gateway to the Rockies for mountain men, pioneers, and later, gold miners. Legendary landmark of the western frontier, Pikes Peak stood as a symbol and a goal in the expanding country. An inspiration to artists, its splendid summit views prompted Catherine Lee Bates to compose "America the Beautiful" in 1893.

John Charles Frémont's flair for the dramatic earned him the nickname "Pathfinder," after James Fenimore Cooper's romantic protagonist. The flamboyant and ambitious topographical engineer (above) actually found few new paths on his five surveying expeditions of the 1840s and 1850s. What he did accomplish was the scientific mapping of these routes. Frémont was an advocate of Manifest Destiny; his well-publicized, rapturous writings lured settlers, such as the Mormons, westward.

against accepting such "simbiles" from competing British traders, unless the Indians wished to "incur the displeasure of their Great American Father." When the corps broke camp in the spring of 1805, they took with them two interpreters, George Drouillard and Toussaint Charbonneau, and Charbonneau's wife, a young Shoshone named Sacagawea. They headed upriver, past the mouth of the Yellowstone to the Great Falls of the Missouri, where they began a series of grueling portages. Ahead of them stood the Rocky Mountains, a barrier they had to cross before the winter snows.

One August day, while following a "handsome bold running Creek" that Lewis mistook for the Columbia River, they saw at a distance a small group of Indians along a trail. Lewis halted his men, unfurled a flag, and marched alone and unarmed toward the Indians.

At first the Indians fled, but soon they allowed Lewis to approach and present gifts. When a large group of mounted warriors approached, Lewis again showed his flag. As his journal describes the meeting, the men "embraced me very affectionately. . . . bothe parties now advanced and we wer all carressed and besmeared with their grease and paint till I was heartily tired of the national hug." To the most important of the warriors, Chief Cameahwait, Lewis presented his flag as "an emblem of peace among whitemen" and a "bond of union between us."

With Shoshone horses and guides, and Sacagawea and her infant, the Corps of Discovery turned northward. September brought eight inches of snow as they traced the ridges of the Nez Percé buffalo trail across the Bitterroot Range of the Rockies. Once over the mountains, they built dugout canoes, for they had found streams that would take them to the Columbia River. They reached it by mid-October.

On his premier expedition, Frémont, finding that emigrants heading west had already "discovered" the Oregon Trail, decided to climb what he wrongly deemed the Rockies' highest peak (left). Exuberantly, he planted an American flag on its narrow summit. In 1898 the United States Post Office depicted the event on a commemorative stamp to promote expansionism. Moving into Spanish territory on his third expedition, Frémont raised this flag (above)—instead of the Stars and Stripes—on California's Gavilan Mountain in 1846. Designed and made by his wife, the flag is decorated with an eagle carrying a peace pipe instead of the traditional olive branch to ensure ready recognition by the Indians.

As the expedition paddled downstream, they stopped now and then to greet groups of Indians. Although Clark distributed presents and smoked with the men, the Indians at first remained fearful; in one lodge, Clark found 32 people "in the greatest agutation, Some crying and ringing there hands." When Sacagawea came ashore, "they imediately all came out and appeared to assume new life, the sight of This Indian woman . . . confirmed those people of our friendly intentions, as no woman ever accompanies a war party of Indians in this quarter."

As the Columbia widened, the expedition moved rapidly. In early

November, from their camp alongside the river, they could hear the breakers of the great estuary. "O! the joy," wrote Clark in his journal.

After a rainy winter in a log palisade on the Columbia's south bank, the corps began its homeward journey. On September 23, 1806, they rowed triumphantly into St. Louis. They had been gone for two years, four months, and nine days.

Jefferson also planned expeditions to determine the poorly defined southwestern boundaries of the Louisiana Purchase. One, led by Lt. Zebulon Pike, set out the year that Lewis and Clark returned. Pike's instructions included the usual advisories about Indians, natural history, mapping, and so forth. They also warned him to avoid Spanish "reconnoitering parties." In fact, a large Spanish patrol was hunting him, and had visited a Pawnee village shortly before Pike arrived there for a council. Pike observed that the Spanish had left several flags in the village, one of which hung at the door of the chief's lodge. The lieutenant demanded that a U. S. flag be flown in its place and cautioned the Indians to "acknowledge their American father." An old Indian reluctantly removed the Spanish flag and exchanged it for an American one, which he raised. But Pike realized that the Indians feared the Spanish, so he returned their flag, on condition that it not be hoisted in the presence of the Americans.

Pike and his men became the first United States expedition to cross the southern Great Plains. At the end of 1806 they wintered on a tributary of the Rio Grande in Spanish territory, where, in the spring, they were arrested by a Spanish cavalry unit and held for several months. Pike protested that he had thought he was on the Red River, but historians suspect that he may have been, perhaps unwittingly, part of a spying foray against the Spanish.

His training in science and surveying won Lt. Charles Wilkes (above) command of the U. S. Exploring Expedition of 1838-1842. His party surveyed 280 islands; mapped 800 miles of Oregon coastline; and, by tracing 1,500 miles of its coast, determined Antarctica to be a continent. An engraving from a Wilkes sketch (opposite) depicts crew members of the flagship Vincennes *cavorting on an "ice island," where they planted a flag.*

Overleaf: "The icebergs," Wilkes wrote, "were covered with penguins" —among the 500 bird species collected by his scientists. In four years the expedition accumulated 4,000 fauna and 50,000 flora specimens, which became part of the Smithsonian Institution's core collection.

A continued legacy of government-sponsored scientific expeditions would carry the American flag many times across the continent, to the ocean depths, and to the moon and beyond. John Quincy Adams, as President and later as a member of Congress, promoted a survey of the South Pacific Ocean. On August 18, 1838, the United States Exploring Expedition set sail from Hampton Roads, Virginia, bound for the South Seas, with instructions "to extend the empire of commerce and science; to diminish the hazards of the ocean, and to point out to future navigators a course by which they may avoid dangers. . . ." The expedition's commander, Lt. Charles Wilkes, was a complicated man. On the one hand intelligent, energetic, and visionary, he was also considered arrogant, stern, even paranoid. "With all his faults," said one of his seamen, Charles Erskine, "he was a true American, and loved dearly the old flag."

The Wilkes expedition carried the Stars and Stripes to Tierra del Fuego, across the South Pacific to Australia, to Antarctica, north to Puget Sound, then eastward to the Indian Ocean, around Africa, and, on June 10, 1842, back to the United States. Aboard ship were nine "scientifics," as the civilian scientists and artists were called.

On the island of Hawaii, in the winter of 1840-41, 16 members of the expedition—with 200 Hawaiian porters—climbed the 13,677-foot peak of Mauna Loa. Seaman Erskine remembers a foot of snow on the volcanic mountain's flanks. With Wilkes working alongside his men, they built shelters of lava block for their instruments, established a camp, and hoisted the

Survey photographer John K. Hillers captured John Wesley Powell with Paiute member Tau-ruv (left), in the Uintah Valley of Utah's Wasatch Mountains. A pioneering ethnologist as well as a geologist, Powell made a serious, ever-respectful study of Indian culture that began with linguistic research. Impatient with interpreters, he gained the Indians' trust by learning their languages, enabling him to gather information about all aspects of their culture. A dedicated champion of Indian rights, Powell was instrumental in founding the Smithsonian Institution's Bureau of Ethnology, a repository for material pertaining to North American Indians. Serving as the bureau's first director from 1879 until his death in 1902, he promoted government-funded fieldwork and expanded the scientific scope of ethnology and anthropology.

This homemade flag (opposite) decorated the Nellie Powell, *one of three boats in Powell's 1871 Colorado River expedition. Powell's brother-in-law, geographer Almon H. Thompson, named the boat after his wife, who made a silk American flag for each dory.*

flag. For three weeks they mapped the caldera and made meteorological, magnetic, and gravity measurements. Wild winds and cold weather reminded some of the men of their time in Antarctica. One night a gale blew for hours, demolishing a shelter and destroying instruments. But, reported Erskine (taking a cue from Francis Scott Key?), "At sunrise we were astonished to behold the Star Spangled Banner still proudly waving."

In addition to charting vast areas of the South Pacific, the Wilkes expedition surveyed much of the Oregon Territory, still uneasily shared by

By Dory Through the Canyon

"...the most sublime spectacle on earth," John Wesley Powell described the canyon through which flowed the wild river that the Indians said could not be run. Undeterred, Powell proceeded with his plan to penetrate the last unknown country in the West, between the Colorado and the upper Green Rivers. On May 24, 1869, just below the railroad crossing at Green River Station, Wyoming, Powell—among the last of the premechanized explorers—nosed four overloaded dories into the shallows, unaware that the mercurial river would hurtle them mercilessly through the canyon for the next 98 days and 1,000 miles.

"What falls there are, we know not; what rocks beset the channel, we know not; what walls rise over the river,

we know not...," wrote Powell, whose sketch inspired this engraving (below). Unprepared for the vagaries of the river and having miscalculated both travel time and provisions, his first expedition suffered capsizings, dangerous portages, imminent starvation, and Indian attacks—and made Powell a hero.

In 1871 he repeated the run, putting in at the same spot with three boats (opposite, bottom)—from left, the *Canonita*, the *Emma Dean*, and the *Nellie Powell*—and an 11-man crew of friends and relatives. Square-sterned with added bulkhead, these redesigned boats offered better buoyancy and protection. Named for his wife, Powell's flagship the *Emma Dean*—shown moored in the Colorado's Marble Canyon (above)—featured a captain's chair lashed midway.

The Colorado River, seen here at Granite Rapids (opposite, top), draws modern explorers—some 22,000 each year—for whom the Grand Canyon ever unfolds its majesty.

New York Herald *journalist Henry Morton Stanley (above) traveled to Africa to interview David Livingstone, the Scottish missionary-explorer who set out to find the Nile's source in 1866 and had not been heard from since. Stanley met up with the ailing Livingstone in 1871 at Ujiji, an Arab trading post (above, right). Arriving with flag and gun salutes, Stanley inquired with his now-famous reserve, "Dr. Livingstone, I presume?" In 1874, sponsored by two newspapers, Stanley returned to explore central Africa's lakes and rivers. He traced the Zaire (opposite)—formerly the Congo—west to the coast.*

Great Britain and the United States. Wilkes determined that Puget Sound offered the best harbor in the region and that the dangerous sandbars and currents at the mouth of the Columbia made the estuary useless as a port. It became clear in Washington that the United States must make good its claim on Puget Sound.

Wilkes divided his men into several surveying parties that spread out along the coast and into the mountains. Erskine's group set up their instruments on shore near the flagship *Vincennes* and soon celebrated Independence Day, 1841. "We commenced at daybreak by firing a national salute of twenty-six guns, one for each State in the Union. . . . The reports of the guns not only astonished the natives, but waked up the red-coats in the fort, who came running up to the observatory. . . . We pointed them to our country's flag, which was so proudly waving in the breeze. . . . They then called us a crew of crazy Americans."

Wilkes led a parade of officers and men, with band, fife and drum, and colors flying. The celebrators roasted an ox, and the usually hard-faced Wilkes appeared with a football, kicking it high in the air with a hearty "Sail in, my shipmates!"

The Wilkes expedition was the largest yet assembled by the United States. Land explorations followed it, perhaps smaller in scale but equally

important to the nation. By 1860 the Army's elite Corps of Topical Engineers had thoroughly studied the American West. Lt. Gouverneur K. Warren compiled their findings in a map judged by William H. Goetzmann to be, after the work of Lewis and Clark, "perhaps the most important map of the West ever drawn."

The years following the Civil War saw the era of the "Great Surveys." Three of the men who dominated the period were civilians—Ferdinand V. Hayden, Clarence King, and John Wesley Powell, the explorer of the Grand Canyon. A fourth, Lt. George M. Wheeler, was the last of the Army survey-ors. Hayden, an enthusiastic explorer since a fossil-hunting trip along the

Clad in homemade polar bear and arctic fox fur clothing, which the Inuit taught him to make, Robert E. Peary (above) stands proud on the Roosevelt's deck. The 186-foot, schooner-rigged steamer fought fog and ice as far north as Ellesmere Island's Cape Sheridan in the Arctic Ocean, where the sea ice finally won, immobilizing the ship for the winter. Crammed with recruits and provisions picked up in Greenland (opposite, top)—including 49 Eskimos, 246 sledge dogs, walrus blubber, and 70 tons of whale meat—the ship reeked with an unforgettable "choking stench," according to the captain, Canadian Bob Bartlett. Matthew Henson, (opposite, bottom) the only African American on the polar team, poses with a musk-ox calf. An expert sledge driver, Henson was nicknamed Maripaluk, or "Kind Matthew," by the Eskimos.

Missouri in 1853, was so well-known by 1870 that Congress gave him financial support for a series of western surveys on which he took agronomists, paleontologists, ornithologists, and other scientists. He also hired a photographer, William Henry Jackson, the first of several to take part in the Great Surveys.

Advances in technology have always aided explorers in the field, but the camera confirmed for Americans at home and in the halls of Congress what their great western domain really looked like. One result was more government support for these explorations. In 1867, Clarence King, a 24-year-old geologist and daredevil who once cornered a grizzly in its den, received a congressional commission to explore a swath of land one hundred miles wide from eastern Colorado to the California border. King and his men endured blinding blizzards and severe heat, and sometimes had little to eat but the flesh of their own starved mules.

From 1867 to 1870, George Wheeler mapped the deserts of the southern Great Basin. In 1871 he crossed Death Valley and Nevada and traveled upriver on the Colorado into the Grand Canyon. His incursions into territory where Hayden, King, and Powell had made their names led to feuds among the explorers. Congress, realizing the folly of extravagant, overlapping surveys, ended the work of Hayden, King, and Wheeler, and in 1879 established the United States Geological Survey, with King and then Powell as directors in the early years.

Congress commissioned Adolphus W. Greely, a National Geographic Society founder, to establish a chain of circumpolar meteorology stations. Greeley's corps of 25 men sailed from Newfoundland in the summer of 1881. For two years, using their Greenland camp as a base, Greely and his

men collected rocks, plants, and animals, explored the terrain, and recorded weather and tidal observations each day. Four members of the expedition carried the flag farther north than it had ever been, but still 440 miles short of the Pole. In 1883 their relief ship failed to arrive, and a tragic winter of sickness and starvation followed. When rescue came the following summer, only seven men were still alive.

Robert Peary, one of the true Arctic pathfinders, had been encouraged by Gardiner Greene Hubbard, the National Geographic Society's first President, to plant the American flag "as far north on this planet as you possibly can!" On Arctic expeditions from 1891 to 1895 he undertook sledge journeys of hundreds of miles, proving Greenland to be an island and not part of a polar landmass. In 1902 he set a farthest-north record for the Western Hemisphere, reaching a point 340 miles from the Pole. In 1906 he surpassed it and photographed two American flags flapping in the wind just

North to the Pole

From their camp at Cape Columbia on Ellesmere Island, Peary's expedition team faced a northward journey of 413 nautical miles over "icy chaos" to the Pole. To move most efficiently across the frozen Arctic, Peary separated the party of 24 men, including 17 Eskimos, plus 19 sledges and 133 dogs, into 7 relay teams. Rotating supporting teams, he theorized, would bear the brunt of the work—depositing provisions, building igloos—in order to conserve the energy of the final assault group. Below, an advance party tackles a pressure ridge, a jumble of pack ice squeezed by wind and tide, sometimes towering 25 feet. The well-packed sledges, each of which held a 50-day supply of tea, biscuits, and pemmican, weighed 500 pounds apiece.

Near the Pole at Camp Jesup (opposite, bottom right), an Eskimo named Egingwah scans the horizon for land, possibly searching for the elusive Crocker Land, a phenomenon dismissed later as an Arctic mirage.

The last support party turned back on April 1, launching the final team—Peary, Henson, 4 Eskimos, and 40 dogs—on its 133-mile push to the Pole. Documenting their arrival on April 6, 1909, Peary photographed his companions (opposite, top) before a polar pressure ridge, in which they planted the flag made by Peary's wife. From it Peary cut a diagonal strip to leave at the Pole, but it eventually disappeared. The taffeta banner (opposite, bottom left), which Peary wore wrapped around his body while in the field, has rectangular patches that indicate the snippets he deposited on earlier expeditions. Some of these were later found. Peary's widow presented the flag to the National Geographic Society in 1955.

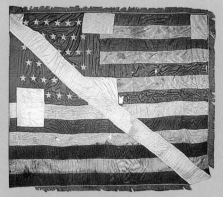

Emblazoned with the Stars and Stripes, Lt. Cmdr. Richard E. Byrd's trimotor Josephine Ford *glides toward the North Pole and the dawn of a new age of polar exploration in N. C. Wyeth's visionary painting of 1926. "The dog sledge must give way to the aircraft; the old school has passed," Byrd declared to an audience at the National Geographic Society in 1926, just after his historic first flight over the North Pole.*

At this latitude, conventional magnetic and gyroscopic compasses became erratic. Taking advantage of the midnight sun, Byrd and his copilot, Floyd Bennett, relied on a sun compass—invented for them by National Geographic's chief cartographer, Albert H. Bumstead—to navigate over the gleaming ice fields. While a sundial indicates time, the sun compass indicates directions by the shadow of the sun.

200 miles from the top of the world. In the intervals between journeys, he wrote, "I began to long for the great white desolation, the battles with the ice and the gales, . . . the silence, the vastness of the great, white lonely North. And back I went. . . ." When Peary finally reached the North Pole on April 6, 1909, he was 52 years old, a veteran of many arduous Arctic explorations.

Admiral Peary spent the last years of his life promoting American aviation from his home in Maine. Six years after his death, Lt. Comdr. Richard E. Byrd wrote in NATIONAL GEOGRAPHIC magazine, "On May 9, 1926, Floyd Bennett and I looked down upon the North Pole from our monoplane, completely verifying Peary's observations, and demonstrating the feasibility of using airplanes in any part of the globe." Byrd brought with him on this flight "a little coin" that Peary had carried to the North Pole. As he circled in the plane, Byrd dropped Peary's medal over the spot.

Aircraft also made possible Byrd's five Antarctic explorations. From late 1928 to 1930, his first expedition, with support from the National Geographic Society and other donors, worked in the south polar region. Among its achievements were the first flight over the South Pole, the discovery of important mountain ranges, the charting of inlets and bays

and vast stretches never before seen by the human eye, and the gathering of meteorological data and a wealth of information on living conditions among fields and cliffs of ice.

On December 25, 1928, the expedition reached the Ross Ice Shelf just off the Antarctic coast. Byrd radioed back home, "On this Christmas

A late-August Antarctic sunrise signaled Byrd's crew to ready the Floyd Bennett, *which had wintered in a canvas-roofed snow pit, for its South Pole flight (opposite). In all, 15,000 pounds of gear—sleeping bags, tents, furs, food, stoves, skis, a sledge, and a mapping camera—were loaded onto the plane. In memory of his friend, who died four months before the expedition, Byrd weighted a flag with a stone from Bennett's grave (above) and later dropped it over the Pole.*

Day we are thankful and proud to report that we have been able to carry the American flag several hundred miles farther south than it has ever been, and it seems fitting that an airplane, that instrument of good-will, should reach its farthest south on Christmas Day."

As never before, the American people were able to share the lives of explorers in the field. Russell Owen of the *New York Times* accompanied Byrd and the 40 other men who wintered in their cramped, half-buried huts at their base, Little America. Owen radioed daily dispatches to his paper. Paramount News cameramen Willard Van der Veer and Joseph Rucker shot 30 miles of movie film. Their footage, plus photography of the polar flight by one of the pilots, Harold June, was distilled into an hour-and-a-half feature, *With Byrd at the South Pole,* a rousing piece of Americana. Moviegoers repeatedly saw the Stars and Stripes whipping in icy winds. They endured the four-month polar night with men who shared family snapshots, worked in the machine shop, packed rations for the scientific teams, read, smoked, argued sometimes, and apologized. They followed the men who made dangerous, difficult forays onto the ice to perform scientific tasks. They rejoiced when the spring sun rose above the horizon and celebrated by raising the American colors, along with British and Norwegian flags in honor of the earlier Antarctic explorers: Scott, Amundsen, Shackleton, and Mawson. Sousa marches animate the sound track at times of triumph, such as Byrd's rescue of his stranded

geological team. "The Star-Spangled Banner" resounds at the precise moment that Byrd and his crew of three fly over the South Pole.

Once explorers had tested their wings, there seemed no limits. By the mid-1940s, Project RAND—a group of engineers working in California—had developed a preliminary design for "a spaceship which will circle the earth as a satellite." The RAND report predicted that the development of such a "craft by the United States would inflame the imagination of mankind. . . ."

But it was the Soviet Union that did it first, launching Sputnik on

October 4, 1957. In 1961, on April 12, Soviet cosmonaut Yuri Gagarin became the first human being to orbit the earth. A few weeks later, President John F. Kennedy called upon America to "commit itself to achieving the goal, before this decade is out, of landing a man on the moon and returning him safely to earth. . . . It will not be one man going to the moon . . . it will be an entire nation."

In the early sixties the Soviet space program kept gaining, always a few steps ahead, with the first successful moon probes, the first space walk, and other feats. But in June 1965 the American Project Gemini launched the first U. S. astronaut to make a space walk. As James McDivitt piloted Gemini 4, orbiting at 18,000 miles an hour, Edward White II opened the hatch and stepped out into space, tethered to a 32-foot "umbilical cord." He maneuvered by means of a hand-held device that squirted jets of compressed gas. His fuel lasted for 20 minutes, when Mission Control ordered him back to the spacecraft.

In December 1965 two more flights brought America closer to meeting President Kennedy's challenge. Astronauts Walter Schirra, Jr., and Thomas Stafford made the first space rendezvous in Gemini 6. In a modern phenomenon unknown to early explorers, they prepared for their mission by training in a simulator—a ground-based duplicate of parts of the spacecraft. Over and over, they practiced each move they would need to make to accomplish the rendezvous safely and successfully.

The ship they were to meet, Gemini 7, went up first, carrying Frank Borman and James A. Lovell, Jr. Schirra and Stafford followed a few days later. Once in orbit, they caught up to Borman and Lovell. At a distance of 1,000 yards, Schirra fired Gemini 6's forward thrusters to

Braced with ice axes, spiked steel boots, and a secured rope on Lhotse's steep face, climbers on America's 1963 Everest expedition (opposite) pause at 25,000 feet for a breath of bottled oxygen before pushing toward the looming south summit. At this elevation the rarefied air's oxygen density is two-fifths that at sea level. This largest expedition ever to tackle Everest included a total of 20 members, 37 Sherpas, and 909 porters, as well as 27 tons of equipment and supplies. Above, James W. Whittaker, the first American to reach Everest's 29,028-foot summit on May 1, 1963, raises his ice ax bearing the Stars and Stripes and the National Geographic Society colors. Behind him Old Glory flaps in the 70-mph summit winds.

Exploration of the Deep

Symbol of the nation's questing spirit, the flag heralds undersea accomplishments by explorers of the ocean's "marvelous nether regions." On August 15, 1934, Old Glory traveled to new depths with oceanographic naturalist William Beebe (below, at right) and inventor Otis Barton (below, center), shown on deck after their record dive. The pair plunged 3,028 feet into the Atlantic near Bermuda in a 2-ton steel bathysphere just 4.5 feet in diameter.

In 1979, on the Pacific floor off Oahu, at a depth of 1,250 feet, marine botanist Sylvia A. Earle (right) clutches

bamboo coral with the pincers of her space-age suit. Behind her undulates a flag attached to the manned submersible *Star II*, to which she is tethered. The pressurized metal armor, containing rebreathing devices and room to write, lets Earle make her historic two-and-a-half-hour solo exploration of the seafloor and surface without decompression.

More reminiscent of science fiction than of science (opposite), a rare giant spider crab steals MiniROVER's spotlights at 450 feet in Japan's Suruga Bay—the little-explored bay at the foot of Mount Fuji noted for its remarkable depth and exotic deep-sea life. One of two remotely operated vehicles used in the 1989 pioneering "fishing" expedition supervised by marine biologist Eugenie Clark, the robot, equipped with mechanical arms, television lenses, and deepwater cameras, surveyed the depths from 180 to 800 feet.

Lifting off with a thunderous blast on February 20, 1962, this Mercury-Atlas 6 rocket hurtled astronaut John Glenn into history as the first American to orbit the earth. One of six Mercury flights, Glenn's voyage launched the Apollo mission, which would reach for the moon. Beside his Apollo 16 module, a buoyant John Young (opposite) literally cannot keep his feet on the ground. At one-sixth his earth weight in the gravity-light lunar environment, Young evinces a true lightness of being as he salutes a flag rigged with metal tubes at the top and side to help simulate a breezy look in this windless realm.

slow the craft, and approached to within a few yards. For hours the two Geminis maneuvered in close formation, then Gemini 6 departed to splash down in the Atlantic.

Gemini 7 stayed aloft for a total of 206 earth orbits. The flights proved that both men and machines were almost ready to plant the flag on the moon. The goal was even closer at the end of 1968. In December, with only a year left on President Kennedy's timetable, the U. S. launched the first manned flight to orbit the moon—Apollo 8, with astronauts Borman, Lovell, and William Anders. On Christmas Eve, as the spacecraft circled the moon, the world watched a television broadcast. Apollo's crew read from the Book of Genesis, and closed their transmission with greetings to "all of you on the good earth."

By this time, the Stars and Stripes had become a seasoned space traveler. Astronauts carried flags to be returned to earth as treasured historic artifacts. Spacecraft and suits bore the emblem. In July 1969, when Apollo 11's *Columbia* roared off the launchpad with astronauts Neil Armstrong, Edwin Aldrin, Jr., and Michael Collins, it carried an American flag that would stand nearly a quarter of a million miles from earth.

Four days after blast-off, the lunar module *Eagle* undocked from its position on *Columbia*'s nose and carried Armstrong and Aldrin to the lunar surface. "Magnificent desolation," Aldrin called it. The two astronauts set up the flag "with some difficulty," Collins later reported, because of "the dense, rocky soil." For two and a half hours *(Continued on page 162)*

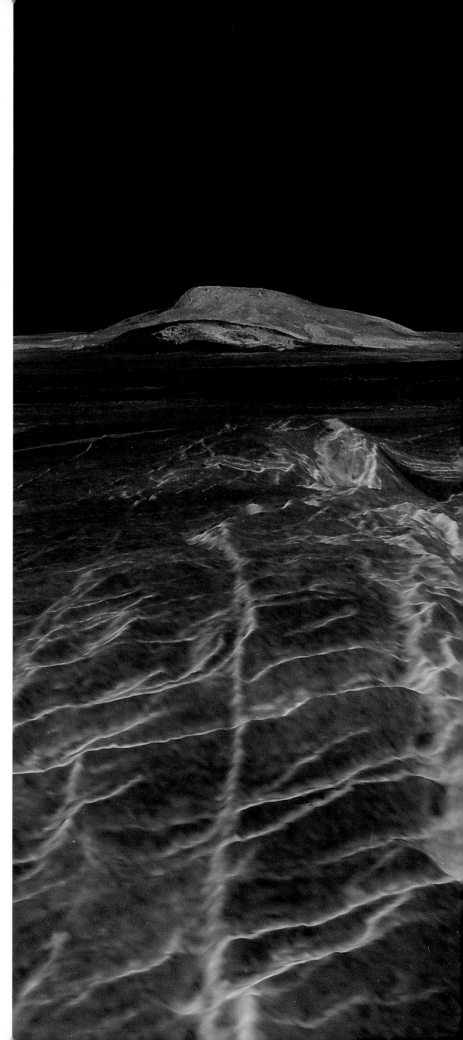

William F. Fisher and James D. A. "Ox" van Hoften (above)—pioneers in the second space age ushered in with the space shuttle—negotiate Discovery's exterior 220 miles above the earth to retrieve a satellite, which the shuttle crew repaired and relaunched. Computer-enhanced images of Venus (right), made from data gathered by the Magellan spacecraft, give earthlings an explorer's perspective of their veiled sister planet without setting foot on its inhospitable surface. This image shows a rift valley slicing the vast lava plain between volcanoes Sif Mons and Gula Mons. Computer-enhanced graphics highlight surface relief and simulate the orange cast of Venus's cloud-filtered sunlight as the human eye would see it.

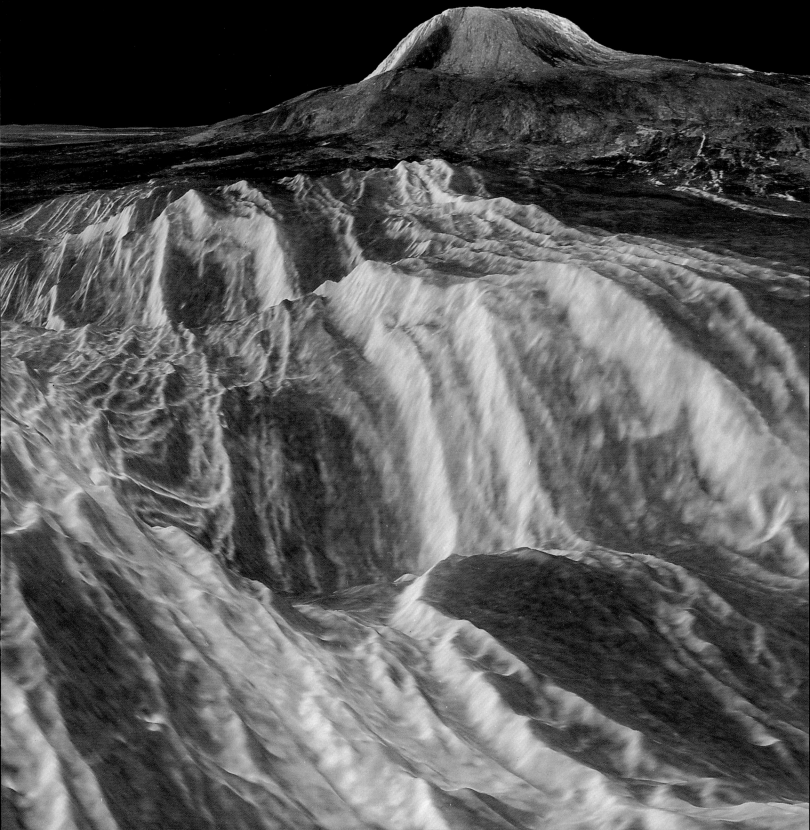

Viewed from Apollo 11, a rising earth, its Pacific and Arctic faces exposed, shines in the lunar sky— a humbling reminder of humankind's fragile place in the universe. "The most significant achievement," wrote editor and essayist Norman Cousins, "was not that man set foot on the Moon, but that he set eye on the Earth."

Armstrong and Aldrin collected moon rocks and arranged scientific instruments to measure seismic activity and other lunar phenomena.

In *Columbia*, Collins circled the moon, two hours per orbit. For 48 minutes of each orbit he crossed the far side, out of touch with earth and with his fellow astronauts. "If a census were taken," he wrote, "there'd be 3 billion plus two on one side, and one plus God only knows what on the other." The next morning, *Eagle* smoothly ascended from its base and docked, and *Columbia* headed home with the jubilant men.

Over the next three years Apollo astronauts made six more moon landings. Planting the flag, Collins has explained, was not a territorial claim but an expression of gratitude for the support of the American people. The flag represented the allegiance of 400,000 engineers, scientists, and others who worked on Project Apollo. At the same time, Collins emphasizes, the view of earth from space is not political—it is global. And the global village shared that perception. Armstrong, Aldrin, and Collins made a round-the-world tour after their flight. "Never did I hear," Collins wrote, "'Well, you Americans finally did it.' Always it was 'we,' we human beings drawn together for one fleeting moment watching two of us walk that alien surface."

Today the American flag regularly goes into space via shuttles and scientific satellites. We look beyond the solar system, into the farthest reaches of space. And we also look back, to study our home planet. Let the visionary Richard E. Byrd speak for explorers of the past, present, and future. In 1928 he wrote, "The urge to go adventuring, to try that which has never been done before, . . . has its meaning—is a part of the scheme of things— and is entwined in the roots of progress."

The Flag in Daily Life

The Flag in Daily Life

We, the people of the United States, fly our flag almost everywhere. It waves over government buildings and country stores, above national shrines and suburban malls. From the huge 90-pound, 20-by-38-foot Army garrison banner to the tiny flag clutched in a child's fist, Old Glory celebrates holidays and ordinary days. We display the flag in schoolrooms, on used-car lots, and—making personal, individual statements of pride—on lawns and front porches across 50 states.

Americans have not always bespangled the landscape with red, white, and blue. During and after the War of 1812, a newly heightened nationalism found expression in parades and flamboyant oratory, but the flag was a far less popular symbol of the country than were images of the bald eagle, George Washington, and the classically robed female figures of Liberty and Columbia. Even so, in May 1812, the people of Colrain, Massachusetts, raised the Stars and Stripes above their log schoolhouse—the first school in the United States to fly the flag.

As the years went by, pride in the flag grew. With the advent of the Civil War, it skyrocketed. In the words of historian George Henry Preble, "When the stars and stripes went down at Sumter, they went up in every town and county in the loyal States. . . . All at once the dear old flag meant the Declaration of Independence; it meant Lexington . . . it meant freedom."

At the same time, Francis Scott Key's anthem rose in popularity. By 1876, as the United States celebrated its Centennial, the "Star-Spangled Banner" was known as "the National Ode" and "the National Hymn," although it had no official status and invariably shared the platform with

A garden-variety snapshot (opposite) captures an uncommon display of Old Glory and a moment of unabashed patriotism. Once an exclusive military and political emblem, the Stars and Stripes had become a fixture in American daily life by the 20th century.

Each day at dawn, innkeeper Jay Schatz displays the Stars and Stripes on the gingerbread-trimmed porch of his historic Abbey Inn (right) in Cape May, New Jersey. Already versed in traditional flag etiquette, young citizens (above) herald and salute the family banner.

Putting aside his cares for an afternoon, Woodrow Wilson throws out the first ball at a 1918 congressional baseball game, in which the Republicans pounded the Democrats, 19-5. His wife, Edith, sits beside him in the flag-draped presidential box. An avid baseball fan, Wilson had a room in his house on S Street he called "the dugout," a special place where he talked about the game with friends. In a solemn moment before a minor league game, a player (opposite) bows his head while he listens to the "Star-Spangled Banner."

"Yankee Doodle," "My Country 'Tis of Thee," and other patriotic airs. In Cincinnati, schoolchildren sang Key's verses, "each member of the chorus waving a flag in time to the music and singing as if life depended on it." The firing of cannon punctuated other Centennial performances of the "Star-Spangled Banner."

By the turn of the century, the U. S. Navy, Marines, and Army prescribed the playing of Key's song as part of various color ceremonies, but still, it was not officially recognized as the national anthem. One reason for the long delay was that the "Star-Spangled Banner" had many critics.

It was too hard to sing, people complained. Also, said one lady, its tune came from "a barroom ballad composed by a foreigner." To some, the words were too militaristic, too narrowly focused on a single event, and conveyed enmity toward Great Britain, with whom we had long been friendly. From time to time, writers—among them Oliver Wendell Holmes—composed new stanzas. On the matter of Key's verses, the *Baltimore Sun* declared the "Star-Spangled Banner" to be "a song of rejoicing for deliverance from a great peril, and a glowing symbolization of our flag as the outward and visible sign of the principles of freedom and justice."

Sporting versions of the flag motif mark America's Olympians as they compete for the gold. Among the nation's best athletes, cyclist David Brinton (left) presses on in the 4,000-meter individual pursuit at the 1988 Seoul Games. In Barcelona (opposite, top), the four-man team of Mike Marsh, Leroy Burrell, Dennis Mitchell, and Carl Lewis embrace after winning the 100-meter relay in 1992. First to finish in the 1992 women's 200-meter final, Gwen Torrence (opposite, bottom) exuberantly closes her victory lap.

During the 1920s, patriotic organizations and individuals sponsored contests for the composition of a national anthem. None of the submissions made the grade. Resolutions and bills to officially adopt the "Star-Spangled Banner" had been introduced in Congress from at least 1913 onward. Finally, on March 3, 1931, the Senate adopted—and President Herbert Hoover signed—the act that gave the United States our official anthem.

Although Holmes's new words for the "Star-Spangled Banner" were

Cooling off in the spray of a fire hydrant, runners celebrate their finish in the Atlanta Peachtree ten-kilometer race on the Fourth of July. In addition to suiting up in red, white, and blue, they sang the "Star-Spangled Banner" while they ran, an endeavor that drew an enthusiastic response from crowds along the route.

The Flag in Daily Life

composed during the Civil War, they carry an ironic significance for other eras as well. In part, Holmes wrote of the flag,

> *If a foe from within strike a blow at her glory,*
> *Down, down with the traitor . . . !*

In the view of many Americans, foes from within have often struck blows at the Stars and Stripes and its traditional ideals. To other citizens, such "blows" constitute justifiable civil disobedience or an exercise of free speech. In an American tradition of antiwar protest that reaches from before the Revolution to the present day, Henry David Thoreau, in 1846, spent a night in jail in Concord, Massachusetts, because he would not pay a tax to support the Mexican War—to him a repugnant, unjust war that would raise the Stars and Stripes over extended slave territory.

On July 4, 1911, the Hedlund family (opposite) gathered on their front porch in St. Paul, Minnesota, for a picnic under the Stars and Stripes. The 21-year-old photographer, Joseph Pavlicek, a recent immigrant from Eastern Europe, was staying with the Hedlunds at the time. He bought the children fireworks to celebrate the holiday, and remembers being so grateful to be living in America that his heart "was nearly bursting." In a more somber mood, six orphans swaddled in an early version of the flag (above) take part in a 1918 pageant in Cooperstown, New York.

"I Pledge Allegiance to the Flag
of the United States of America
and to the Republic for which it stands
one Nation under God, indivisible,
with liberty and justice for all."

In honor of the Columbus quadricentennial, the Boston-based children's weekly, *The Youth's Companion*, published a few words on September 8, 1892, for students to repeat on Columbus Day that year: *"I pledge allegiance to my Flag and the Republic for which it stands—one nation indivisible—with liberty and justice for all."*

Controversy surrounded the question of who actu-

ally wrote the original pledge, with claims made by descendants of James Upham and Francis Bellamy, both former magazine employees. It took a committee of the U. S. Flag Association to determine once and for all in 1939 that Bellamy (above), the circulation manager and a native of Rome, New York, had indeed written the lines.

Reprinted on thousands of leaflets, the pledge went out to public schools across the country. On October 12, 1892, more than 12 million children marked the 400th anniversary of Columbus's arrival by reciting for the first time a pledge of allegiance to the Stars and Stripes, in all its unstandardized glory, instituting what would become a required school-day ritual in many states. Nearly 50 years later, students at a southern elementary school (opposite) salute the flag during a pledge ceremony.

On June 14, 1923, at the first National Flag Conference in Washington, D. C., an editorial change was made. The words "the flag of the United States" replaced "my flag," conferees reasoning that this would keep immigrants from drifting to thoughts of their native colors when they recited the pledge.

In the years following, other modifications were suggested, but never formally adopted: adding an oath to abstain from drinking alcohol, substituting the phrase "born

and unborn" at the end of the pledge, and making it clear that "liberty and justice for all" is a goal rather than an established fact.

In June 1943, one year after the Pledge of Allegiance was officially recognized by Congress, the Supreme Court ruled that schoolchildren could not be forced to recite it. A last amendment was made in June 1954, when the words "under God" were added. "In this way," said then-President Dwight D. Eisenhower, "we are reaffirming the tran-

scendence of religious faith in America's heritage and future; in this way we shall constantly strengthen those spiritual weapons which forever will be our country's most powerful resource in peace and war."

Cowboys display proper flag etiquette as they repeat the pledge, a traditional rodeo opener (opposite, left). According to the Flag Code, a man out of uniform should remove his hat with his right hand and hold it over his heart as he faces the flag.

During the Civil War, Holmes's friend John Greenleaf Whittier mythologized another protester. Whittier's poem tells of Confederate Gen. Stonewall Jackson leading his troops into Frederick, Maryland, in 1862, past the house of the 90-year-old widow, Barbara Frietchie, where a Union flag hung from the attic window. Jackson ordered the flag shot down. Barbara Frietchie "snatched the silken scarf," and waved it at Jackson:

> *"Shoot, if you must, this old gray head,*
> *But spare your country's flag," she said.*

A shamed Jackson relented:

> *"Who touches a hair of yon gray head*
> *Dies like a dog! March on!" he said.*

A woman named Barbara Frietchie did live in Frederick at the time. Some of her contemporaries supported the story, although with considerable variation in detail, and there was at least one other claimant for the honor of

upholding the Stars and Stripes on that occasion. Others disputed it, among them one of Jackson's officers, who wrote that Barbara Frietchie "never saw Stonewall Jackson and he never saw her." Accurate or not, the tale seized the American imagination, and, by 1876, a Philadelphia newspaper contended, "There is no Barbara Frietchie for whom the world cares a fig, except the Barbara Frietchie of Mr. Whittier."

With an ardor resembling the Widow Frietchie's, various states began to pass laws against damaging or destroying the flag. A further swell of patriotism led to the first national observance of Flag Day, in 1877. Although Presidents Wilson in 1916 and Coolidge in 1927 proposed Flag Day, it was not until 1949, under President Truman, that Congress recognized the anniversary of the adoption, on June 14, 1777, by the Continental Congress, of the Stars and Stripes as the official flag of the United States of America.

Schools taught the rituals and principles of citizenship. A teachers' manual published in 1901 outlined patriotic exercises and tableaux in honor of heroes from George Washington to Theodore Roosevelt. In one program, "six wee maidens," dressed alternately in red, white, and blue, march to a stirring air, wave small flags, and speak lines that begin, "Be brave like Washington." In another, ten boys perform a drill in honor of the "starry emblem," recite a poem, and close with three cheers for the "Red, White, and Blue."

Adults, too, participated in patriotic programs. Franklin K. Lane, Secretary of the Interior, delivered a 1914 Flag Day address in which he repeated

Champion bugler Adrian Fredericks (opposite) plays taps into the microphone of radio station WJZ as part of a drive to recruit a thousand new troop leaders for the Boy Scouts of America.

Each year, thousands of towns across the country put on their own Memorial Day parades to honor the men and women who have given their lives for their country in war. In Salisbury, Connecticut, Brownie Scouts (above) prepare to greet an approaching parade with their own diminutive Stars and Stripes.

Long regarded as dependents incapable of making their own political decisions, women had to fight strong opposition to win suffrage. In 1920, after more than 40 years of agitation and debate, Congress ratified the 19th Amendment, which gave women the right to vote. The year the amendment was written into law, many women cast their first ballots in a presidential election (above). Taking part in a women's suffrage meeting (right), young girls looked ahead to the time when they themselves would be eligible to vote—perhaps even for female candidates. When the 19th Amendment was passed, suffrage organizer Carrie Chapman Catt cautioned that real progress depended on women winning powerful political offices. "If you really want women's votes to count," she said, "make your way there."

On April 5, 1976, a white high school student, one of 200 anti-busing demonstrators in Boston that day, used the flag as a lance to lunge at a black attorney who walked onto the scene.

Holding the flag high as a banner for his cause, a marcher (opposite) makes his way along the road from Selma to Montgomery, Alabama, in the spring of 1965, protesting continued efforts to deny most southern blacks their rights to register and vote. Within months of the march, Congress approved the Voting Rights Act of 1965.

words he said the flag had spoken to him that morning: "I am what you make me; nothing more. I swing before your eyes as a bright gleam of color, a symbol of yourself."

Another kind of "human flag" has become a tradition observed over generations in Fort McHenry's Living Flag Ceremony. In 1985 an 82-year-old Maryland woman attended Fort McHenry's festivities—where some 3,000 schoolchildren, lining up as stripes or stars, held aloft placards of red, white, and blue—and proudly reported that in 1914 she had been one of thousands of children to form a living Star-Spangled Banner on the same lawns of the fort.

Also in 1914, President Wilson approved a congressional resolution

Teenagers when this photograph was taken in 1908, identical twins Yansci and Rozicka (opposite), known as the "Dolly Sisters," were already a much celebrated act in American vaudeville. Born in Hungary and raised on New York's Lower East Side, the sisters were famous for their acrobatic dances and fabulous costumes— Greek robes, fringed dresses, and even Star-Spangled Banners.

Overleaf: In 1942, while America waged war in Europe, Warner Bros. produced the film Yankee Doodle Dandy, *a musical biography loosely based on the life of American composer George M. Cohan. James Cagney played the patriotic songwriter, a role that won him an Academy Award for Best Actor. In the theme song, Cohan proudly claims to be "a real live nephew of my Uncle Sam's—Born on the Fourth of July!"*

asking the American people "to display the Flag at their homes or other suitable places on the second Sunday in May, as a public expression of our love and reverence for the mothers of our country." Women who had lost sons and daughters in World War I and—later—in World War II were known as Gold Star Mothers, after the small banners they hung in the windows of their houses. In 1936, President Roosevelt called the Stars and Stripes to this cause as well, designating the last Sunday in September as Gold Star Mothers' Day, and asking people to fly the flag and to honor the "supreme sacrifice of motherhood" these women had made.

Both of these flag resolutions described American mothers as "the greatest source of the country's strength" and "the home as the fountainhead of the state." They praised the contributions of women to "religion, hence . . . good government and humanity."

Clearly the flag had become enshrined as the country's supreme symbol, guardian of everything from apple pie to the entire human race. Patriotic organizations developed standards for usage and display of the symbol, but only in 1942 did Congress enact a national flag code. It carried no penalties for ignoring the rules.

In the 1960s things changed. A counterculture, composed mostly of young people, began to express itself loudly. In resistance to the values of established society, the counterculture seized the supreme symbol of the establishment, heating up a struggle for control of the flag and its message. Flags were cut into bits and pieces, patched to jeans and coveralls. Activist Abbie Hoffman used a flagkerchief to blow his nose during public presentations. During these chaotic years, flag sales soared. Flag decals by

Released in 1969, **Easy Rider** *was the first major film to focus on the American counterculture. In it, three dropouts (Dennis Hopper, Jack Nicholson, and Peter Fonda, above) journey on motorcycles through scenes filled with drugs, violence, and rock music. One year later, the film* Patton *won eight Academy Awards for its epic portrayal of the career of George S. Patton, a highly successful and controversial general in World War II. In the opening scene (opposite), Patton (George C. Scott) delivers a speech that celebrates the glories of war.*

the thousand popped up on the car windows of Americans angered by what they saw as counterculture depredation. One taunt proclaimed: "America—love it or leave it."

Loving America was exactly what it was all about—each in his or her own way. College students and other citizens across the country challenged America's escalating role in Vietnam, in what they believed to be a dishonorable war. In August 1968 streets outside the Democratic convention hall in Chicago became the scene of violent battles between antiwar protesters and police. Flags went up in flames.

By this time, a federal law was on the books. It forbade "publicly mutilating, defacing, defiling, burning, or trampling upon" the flag, and

The flags of Britain, France, and the United States decorate New York's Fifth Avenue in Childe Hassam's painting "Allies Day, May 1917." Soon after the United States entered World War I, the city officially welcomed war commissioners from Britain and France with parades and a colorful show of solidarity.

"America, America," painted by John Nieto, pays tribute to the tenacity and endurance of Native Americans. Dressed in plains leggings and a warrior's choker, and draped in the Stars and Stripes, Nieto's Indian stands defiant. "I see him a bit like a fortress that has survived 500 years of cultural bombardment," says the artist, who is himself of Spanish and Indian descent.

prescribed fines and imprisonment. Challenges soon came. A man in Washington, D. C., tore a flag, and a woman in Arizona burned one. Although lawyers argued that the flag law infringed upon First Amendment guarantees of free speech, and that such actions were symbolic speech, the courts upheld the flag desecration law.

The Vietnam War ended in 1975. With the Bicentennial celebrations of 1976, the nation came together under the Stars and Stripes, as it did in late 1979, when Iranian revolutionaries attacked the American Embassy in Tehran, seized more than 50 hostages, and burned the flag in front of news cameras. Only as President Carter left office, in January 1981, did Iran release the hostages. They came home to cheering crowds and a riot of red, white, and blue. Once again, Americans saw the flag as the symbol that gave coherence, structure, and unity to our national identity.

The desecration issue came to a head again in the late 1980s. One forum was the Art Institute of Chicago, where a short-lived exhibit bore the title "What Is the Proper Way to Display a U. S. Flag?" Part of the artwork consisted of a shelf with a ledger for viewers to write answers to the question. Spread on the floor directly below the shelf, exactly where a person would have to stand to write in the ledger, lay Old Glory.

Flag-waving, sign-bearing protesters besieged the gallery. Inside, war veterans repeatedly removed the flag from the floor, and spoke their minds. "The red stripes," said one, "stand for the blood of the men who died for that flag." Another declared, "The flag is a symbol. Without symbols, how will we know who we are?"

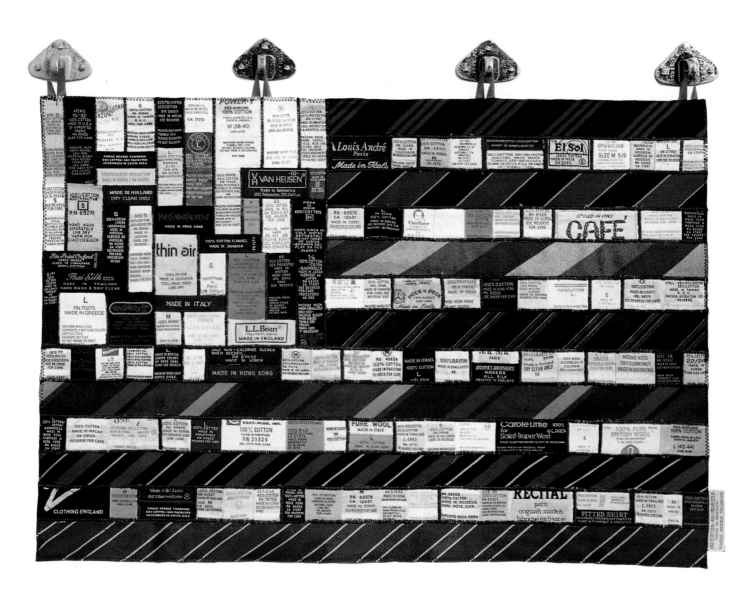

Artist Kim Abeles created "Made in America" as part of an exhibit of new flags for presidential election year 1992. To make this patchwork banner, she collected manufacturing labels from the clothing of four people and stitched them together with remnants of neckties. Some 50 foreign countries are represented in all.

In June 1989 the Supreme Court heard the appeal of a man who had burned a flag and been convicted under a Texas flag desecration law. The Court considered whether or not the conviction was in violation of the First Amendment, and decided that it was. Writing for the majority, Justice William Brennan said, "We can imagine no more appropriate response to burning a flag than waving one's own, no better way to counter a flag-burner's message than by saluting the flag that burns, no surer means of preserving the dignity even of the flag that burned than by—as one witness here did—according its remains a respectful burial. We do not consecrate the flag by punishing its desecration, for in doing so we dilute the freedom that this cherished emblem represents."

In his dissent, Chief Justice William Rehnquist invoked military heroes and "200 years of history" and quoted the "Star-Spangled Banner," "Barbara

Frietchie," and a verse from Ralph Waldo Emerson's "Concord Hymn."

Congress again took the legislative route and passed a new Flag Protection Act. Again, protesters across the country contested it. On October 30, 1989, the day after the law went into effect, four men were arrested for flag burning on the steps of the U. S. Capitol. Their case, too, ended up in the Supreme Court, which overturned the statute in June 1990, invalidating all of the nation's flag desecration prohibitions on the grounds that they violated the First Amendment.

In both cases, Justice John Paul Stevens dissented. In 1989 he declared that to sanction "the public desecration of the flag will tarnish its value. . . ." But one might ask: Is it possible that the legions of Americans who direct their righteous indignation against flag desecration do so not because burning diminishes the power of the flag— *(Continued on page 200)*

In "Three Flags," painted in 1958, Jasper Johns reduced the symbol of a nation to a series of bold patterns, challenging viewers to look at the flag in a new way. The painting depicts the 48-star flag, which officially flew from July 4, 1912, to July 3, 1959, making it the longest-lived version of the Stars and Stripes.

Art For the People, By the People

The spirit of a nation finds unique expression in the traditional, or folk, art of its people. Idiosyncratic as the artists themselves, these star-spangled objects of Americana, some decorative and some utilitarian, reflect popular, down-home values and reinforce the common bond between maker and viewer.

Generated by the 1876 Centennial Exhibition in Philadelphia, a wave of patriotism swept the United States during the last quarter of the 19th century and into the 20th, touching folk artists as well. Old Glory, that quintessential symbol of Americanism, became the motif of the day—and appeared in an impressive number of forms.

This flag gate (below), salvaged from the Darling farm in Jefferson County, New York, dates to about 1876.

Mounted on metal, the 56-inch-wide, painted wooden banner—its stripes rippled for a breezy effect—once lent a proud and patriotic accent to the farmer's homestead.

Uncle Sam was born during the War of 1812 and matured, in Lincoln's image, with the onset of Centennial fever at the pen of political cartoonist Thomas Nast. A 36-foot-tall fiberglass version (above) greets visitors at Magic Forest Amusement Park in Lake George, New York. The character's real-life namesake, Samuel Wilson, hailed from nearby Troy.

Between 1880 and 1920 an unknown wood-carver

from the Northeast envisioned America's favorite uncle atop a whirligig (above), pedaling a bicycle. The tail banner sports the American flag on one side and the Canadian on the other, perhaps indicating that the toymaker lived near the border between the two countries.

A state is born! proclaims this all-American crib quilt from the Sunflower State (left). Hand-dyed and homespun, appliquéd and pieced, it was made around 1861, the year Kansas joined the Union and the flag gained its 34th star. In addition to statehood celebrations, events such as campaigns, expositions, and even wars often occasioned the making of commemorative quilts seasoned with patriotic motifs.

Gen. James A. Garfield's words, "For love of country they accepted death . . . and made immortal their patriotism and virtue," echoed nearly a century later when John F. Kennedy was assassinated on November 22, 1963. Following ceremonies in the Capitol Rotunda (right), Jacqueline Kennedy and her daughter, Caroline, kneel before the President's flag-draped casket. As specified by the Flag Code, the union must be placed over the head and left shoulder. At Arlington National Cemetery (opposite)—612 Virginia acres reserved for burial of military personnel and civil servants— servicemen gave Mrs. Kennedy the folded flag.

Overleaf: On Memorial Day—first observed in 1868, when Civil War graves were decorated on the grounds of Arlington Cemetery—modern-day veterans in Angel Fire, New Mexico, transport a truly Grand Old Flag to a memorial chapel.

In Nevada, a vintage Buick (above) gets a lift from its civic-spirited coat of paint, while in San Francisco (above, right), a brotherly effort inspired this pop-artful flag of hot dogs and popcorn.

Opposite, top: A Maryland tobacco farmer graphically proclaims his support of U. S. troops during the war in the Persian Gulf. At Albuquerque's 1983 International Balloon Fiesta, a hot-air balloon (bottom) displays a lofty show of stars and stripes.

how could it for someone who loves it?—but because they share the anxiety voiced by the veteran in Chicago: "Without symbols, how will we know who we are?"

Under the Star-Spangled Banner, the most diverse groups have claimed their right to the symbol of the flag, have marched and affirmed their identity as Americans, have said, in one way or another, that it belongs to all of us. Pacificists and militarists, radical labor agitators and hard-hatted conservatives have carried the flag, as have the Ku Klux Klan and civil rights demonstrators, Republicans and Democrats, Whigs, Socialists, Know-Nothings, Wide-Awakes, Free Soilers, Populists, Anti-Masons, Mugwumps, Copperheads, Bull Moosers . . . political parties all, in a country well-known for the ballyhoo with which it elects its Presidents.

Andrew Jackson's 1828 presidential campaign was one of the most significant events in our history. From it grew much of the political style we know today—or did, at least, until the reign of television. By Jackson's time, almost all electors were chosen by voters, rather than by state legislators; Jackson, more than any President before him, entered the White House elected by the power of the people.

It was a landslide victory, due partly to Jackson's enthusiastic support-

ers in the new western states—Old Glory, in 1828, bore 24 stars, the latest honoring Missouri's 1821 statehood. Credit for getting out the Jackson vote goes to his well-organized Democratic Party workers. Flags, banners, and martial music enlivened parades and barbecues modeled on Fourth of July festivities. From Jackson's military feats, and his nickname "Old Hickory," his supporters created an image with an appeal that was not rational, but intensely emotional. During Jackson's second successful campaign, the first national nominating conventions took place. The Anti-Masonic Party led off, in September 1831, followed by the National Republicans three months later, and the Jacksonian Democrats in May 1832. The pattern was set.

Seldom has America—or the rest of the world, for that matter—seen a

Patriotic chic, circa 1919: A young woman models a straw hat embellished with grosgrain ribbon and 48 embroidered stars. A major design house offered this hat for sale in the hope that other Americans would be inspired by this young woman's patriotic spirit.

political campaign the likes of that waged in 1840 by the Whig, William Henry Harrison. The Whigs packaged and sold Harrison, another military hero, as a simple farmer, the "Log Cabin Candidate," although he came from a prominent Virginia family and was born on a Tidewater plantation. Mile-long Harrison parades rolled through cities with flag-bedecked bandwagons that carried log cabin emblems. From rally to rally, Harrison supporters trundled huge, slogan-laden paper or leather balls, coining the phrase "keep the ball rolling." Promises of government reform and barrels of free cider attracted crowds of thousands. Souvenirs—from medals to snuffboxes to

Spoofing Uncle Sam, Frank Zappa wears a top hat decorated with stars and stripes. In the late sixties, Zappa and his band, the Mothers of Invention, were known for offbeat live performances that invited audience participation. The New York Times *once described Zappa as "the Orson Welles of Rock."*

banners and bandannas—bore mottos, eagle emblems, portraits of Harrison, and the log cabin motif. Harrison banners simulated actual flags, although the proportions varied. In the canton, stars—usually 12—encircle a large star, in a year when the stars on the Stars and Stripes numbered 26.

For the next election, the Whigs opened another rousing campaign in Baltimore, with Henry Clay as their candidate. A 42-foot-high arch surmounted by flags spanned a main street. On exhibit, as part of the festivities, was the original Fort McHenry Star-Spangled Banner. Both Clay and his opponent, the victor-to-be, James K. Polk, had flag banners with their

In the spirit of Independence Day, an onlooker at a Fourth of July parade (above) flaunts her patriotism, sixties-style, with wig and accessories in a flag motif. A biker and his Harley (opposite) make a striking statement in red, white, and blue during 1965 Bike Week in Daytona Beach, Florida.

Overleaf: Strung across the facade of Amoskeag Mill in Manchester, New Hampshire, an enormous flag measuring 50 by 95 feet makes lilliputians of local textile-mill workers posing in 1917.

names, slogans, portraits, and emblems—Clay's was a raccoon—spread across field or canton. One Polk flag featured, in the canton, the candidate's portrait ringed by stars. Outside the canton, on a white stripe, was a single blue star that stood for Texas. It also represented Polk's desire to annex that territory and thereby win southern votes.

As the century approached its midpoint, a small, secretive political group named itself the Order of the Star Spangled Banner. It grew into the American Party and launched its anti-immigrant, anti-Catholic campaign. Soon the nation was calling the group the Know-Nothings because, when questioned about their beliefs, members replied, "I know nothing." The Know-Nothings pledged to make immigrants wait 21 years for naturalization, and to bar the foreign born and Catholics from holding office. They hired thugs called Plug-uglies to shoot at and terrorize unsympathetic voters. Like other parties, the Know-Nothings waved the flag. One of their banners bears a portrait of their adopted hero, George Washington.

The Republican nominee in 1856 was the explorer John Charles Frémont. His campaign employed old-style parades, the log cabin symbol, and starred-and-striped flag banners in a multitude of variations. One red-and-gold-fringed banner depicts "the brave path finder" atop a needle-peaked mountain, planting not his eagle flag, nor the 26-star, 1842 flag he would have had on his first western expedition, but the 1856 flag of 31 stars.

When Abraham Lincoln led the Republican Party to victory in 1860, his supporters wielded split rails and wooden axes, the rails sometimes regarded as holy relics split by the young Lincoln himself. In this contest, all parties made abundant use of flag-imitating banners, with candidates' names sprawling across the stripes. One red-and-white- *(Continued on page 208)*

Amid mounds of stripes and stars, skilled employees at Annin & Company in Roseland, New Jersey—flag makers since 1847 and the world's largest supplier today—put the finishing touches on flags by hand.

The world's largest flag (opposite), made by Humphrys Flag Company in Pottstown, Pennsylvania, measures 255 by 505 feet—the size of 3 football fields—and weighs more than a ton. Unfurled on Flag Day, 1992, the banner used 5.5 miles of fabric and 6,000 miles of thread.

striped banner with no names or slogans, featured instead of stars in the canton, a pensive, tousle-headed, beardless Lincoln.

Elaborately uniformed groups calling themselves Wide-Awakes marched in Republican parades, flying flags and carrying signs with their emblem, a wide-open eye. Brightly blazing torches became a Wide-Awake trademark, as did the oilcloth capes the marchers wore to protect themselves from drips of torch oil. In Chicago, 10,000 Wide-Awakes paraded in their martial drills to the music of 43 bands. In New York, 12,000 gathered, and *Harper's Weekly* and *Leslie's* published engravings of the thrilling torchlight processions.

Political banners that mimicked the Stars and Stripes were in use for many years, but they gradually disappeared. In 1868 the Republican candidate Ulysses S. Grant protested the defacing of flags for political gain: "There is no name so great that it should be placed upon the flag of our country." When William McKinley conducted his 1896 front-porch campaign from

Electric guitarist Jimi Hendrix delivered a haunting interpretation of the national anthem at the close of Woodstock, the historic three-day music festival that brought half a million people to White Lake, New York, in the summer of 1969. Abbie Hoffman (above, right), a former pharmaceutical salesman turned radical activist, was a master at using symbols to challenge authority. In 1968 he was arrested on flag desecration charges for wearing a store-bought flag shirt to hearings before the House UnAmerican Activities Committee.

his home in Canton, Ohio, he greeted voters with Old Glory flying in the yard. Emulating McKinley's successful strategy, Warren G. Harding, 24 years later, received visitors—including celebrities such as Al Jolson—from his Marion, Ohio, front porch. On the lawn was the flagpole that had stood at McKinley's home, with a 48-star flag rippling in the breeze.

In his campaign speeches, Harding challenged his listeners to "exalt America first!" As an 11-year-old Ohio farm boy, Harding had seen his compatriots exalt America to the utmost. It was 1876, the hundredth anniversary of the Declaration of Independence, America's birthday, and the occasion for extravaganzas of flag-waving and self-congratulation.

People welcomed the Centennial year all across the Republic. Philadelphia—the site of Independence Hall, where Congress had adopted the Declaration—threw the biggest party. It began on New Year's Eve, with bells, whistles, pistol shots, the "Star-Spangled Banner," torches, and fireworks. Of the just-past American century, the New York *Herald* declared that it had "been the most fruitful and the most glorious period of equal length in the history of the human race."

To celebrate the country's achievements, Philadelphia held a world's fair, the Centennial Exhibition, which would draw 10 million visitors in a nation of some 46 million people. For the May 10 opening, Philadelphia citizens decorated their houses with flags and bunting. Hundreds of banners

Demonstrators at a Veterans Day Parade in New York City (left) burn the Stars and Stripes to protest the Flag Protection Act of 1989, a federal law that made it a criminal act to burn or defile the flag. Many Americans saw such a law as a violation of their right to free speech. "Liberty needs special protection," said one American Civil Liberties Union director, "not its symbol . . . ." Another protester, railing against the law he interpreted as enforced patriotism, put a gag in his mouth and let his sign do all the talking.

and flags—from the Stars and Stripes to flags of foreign nations, regimental colors, and naval pennants—adorned the Exhibition buildings.

For the fair, California moved a venerable grapevine from Santa Barbara to Philadelphia. Supported on latticework in its new home, the vine spread across 12,000 square feet. From Iowa, a row of dirt-filled glass columns, four to six feet tall, revealed the richness of the prairie soil. People gazed at

Benjamin Franklin's printing press, George Washington's coat, vest, and breeches. They saw Brazilian cotton, German wine, Egyptian saddles, Danish furs, and shocking nude paintings from France.

When Alexander Graham Bell demonstrated his telephone, a New York reporter asked, "Of what use is such an invention?" In Machinery Hall, *Atlantic Monthly* editor William Dean Howells—and almost everyone else—admired the 40-foot-high steam engine designed by the American inventor George Corliss. "An athlete of steel and iron," Howells called the titan. Its beams rising and falling, the Corliss hummed steadily (its boilers were outside the building) as it powered machines that sawed logs, printed wallpaper, made shoes, spun cotton, and folded paper into envelopes.

In a *Harper's Weekly* cartoon, Brother Jonathan—an Uncle Sam-like personification of the United States— *(Continued on page 222)*

On the campaign trail through the western states in 1903 (opposite), Republican presidential hopeful Teddy Roosevelt soft-pedaled his progressive platform in New Castle, Wyoming, from a podium festooned with bunting and cluttered with symbols of the wilderness—a nod to his conservationist sympathies.

Bipartisan preference for red, white, and blue prevailed at the 1960 Democratic convention (left) in Los Angeles, where John F. Kennedy won the presidential nomination on the first ballot and opened the New Frontier.

Overleaf: At the 1992 Democratic Convention in New York City, delegates celebrate the passing of the torch to nominee Bill Clinton as the new leader of his party. Complementing the rampant tricolor motif, clouds of multicolored balloons released from the ceiling reflect the contemporary face of the party as well as that of the nation.

The Flag and Political Paraphernalia

When it comes to flag waving, there's no time like a presidential campaign, and there's nothing like the paraphernalia of politics for exploiting Old Glory. Historically, its colors and elements have graced campaign media as decorative patriotic symbols.

At the turn of the century, when candidates had to carry their platform directly to the voters, campaign posters, such as that of Democratic hopeful William Jennings Bryan (below), featured allegories, slogans, and vignettes to

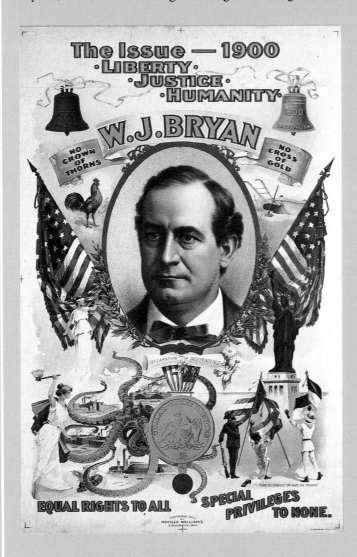

represent the candidate. The hoopla of conventions tends to inspire more outlandish politicking, like that of a delegate at the 1976 Republican Convention (above), who wears his sentiment for Gerald Ford on his hat.

Whig candidate William Henry Harrison promoted his winning frontiersman image in 1840 with a campaign song, "General Harrison's Log Cabin March," featuring a lithograph (opposite, top left) on the song-sheet cover.

A paper-thin lantern (opposite, top right) characterizes Republican Rutherford B. Hayes's lean victory in the electoral college. Not so lucky, Kansas governor and Sunflower State nominee Alfred M. Landon lost in 1936, despite his catchy button (opposite, middle left).

An American flag (opposite, middle right) advertised Abraham Lincoln's aspirations during the 1860 campaign. A simple button (opposite, bottom) represented Democratic hopefuls Walter Mondale and running mate Geraldine Ferraro in 1984.

"One flag, one land, one heart, one hand, One Nation, evermore!" Oliver Wendell Holmes's words sing praise to the Union, celebrated with pomp every four years on Inauguration Day—when Americans, regardless of political persuasion, observe the peaceful transfer of power and renew their faith in the democratic process. Dressed for the occasion, the west facade of the Capitol wears bunting and huge banners hung according to specification, with the union uppermost and to the observer's left.

Overleaf: In February 1981 the Stars and Stripes waves above a throng of New Yorkers celebrating the homecoming of American hostages from Iran. Symbol of solidarity in crisis as well as in resolution, the flag flew profusely across the country in a national show of concern and outrage throughout the 443-day ordeal.

Unfettered as birds on the wing of Old Glory, skydiving Golden Knights (opposite) free-fall at 125 miles an hour some 6,000 feet above the Yuma, Arizona, proving ground for the U. S. Army's parachute team. Strictly an aerial photo mission, the skydive ends 2,000 or 3,000 feet above the ground, when parachutes are released for the homestretch.

welcomed foreign dignitaries to the Centennial Exhibition, and invited them to return in 1976, to see "how big we will be." They would have found a very different celebration. In the 1970s, the goal of officials planning the Bicentennial was to ensure that the nation's birthday party would bring Americans together—"dissidents as well as neighbors and friends."

Across the country, the celebrations took a variety of forms. Some were untraditional and very characteristic of the 1970s. Protesters against everything from oil company profits to the defamation of American Indians enlivened a reenactment of the Boston Tea Party. Cities created gardens and plazas on vacant lots. Communities undertook historic preservation projects.

Everywhere were pomp and parades, speeches and fireworks. Philadelphia's Fourth of July parade took six hours to pass by any group of flag-waving spectators. In Washington, D. C., Americans celebrated their heritage as costumed Greeks, Koreans, Czechs, and Slovaks marched with a multitude of other ethnic groups. In every state, Americans marched in patriotic tribute. Over them all waved the Star-Spangled Banner.

The journey of our country's flag, from the pine trees and rattlesnakes and Continental Colors of the Revolution to today's 50 stars that salute our 50 states, has been a long one, sometimes painful, but most often joyous. The "new constellation" of 1777 still pledges the eternal dawning of a free and fearless new world. All across the land, Francis Scott Key's "broad stripes and bright stars" color American life. Whatever meanings our minds may ascribe to our flag, the same elements are there for us all, for our eyes to *see*: the stripes, bold and true; stripes that by their very form dispel doubt and inspire strength; and the stars, lights shining in the darkness, bright points to infinity, full of promise.

Flag Etiquette

The sight and sound of the Star-Spangled Banner snapping in the wind outside public schools and post offices, over war memorials and athletic fields, daily remind Americans of their national heritage. And each day in every town and city, Americans hoist the flag at sunrise, lower it at sunset, and fold it for safekeeping.

In 1923, at a national conference on flag etiquette in Washington, D. C., participants declared that the flag "represents the living country and is itself considered as a living thing." So that citizens would know how to care for and display the flag properly, Congress adopted the Flag Code of 1942. The code describes the rules and customs surrounding

flag use. Those most commonly referred to are given here. The important thing to remember is that the flag, as a symbol of the nation, should be treated with respect and dignity.

The flag is usually flown outside from sunrise to sunset; if displayed at night, it should be properly illuminated. All-weather flags should be flown in inclement weather. The flag should be hoisted with dispatch and lowered with ceremony. When not in use, it should be folded properly for storage.

To fold the flag, hold it waist-high with another person so that its surface is parallel to the ground. Fold the lower half of the stripe section lengthwise over the field of stars, holding the bottom and top edges securely. Fold the flag again lengthwise. Make a triangular fold by bringing the striped corner of the folded edge to meet the open edge. Turn the outer point inward, parallel to the open edge, to form a second triangle, and repeat along the length of the flag. When the flag is completely folded, only a triangular blue field of stars should be visible.

When the flag is displayed on a wall (FIG. 1), either horizontally or vertically, the field of stars should be in the uppermost corner on the flag's right (the observer's left).

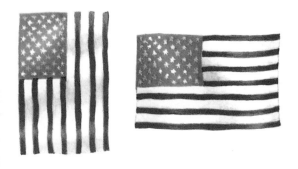

(FIG. 1) *Displayed on a wall*

(FIG. 2) *In procession, carried either on marchers' right or at front and center*

(FIG. 3) *On a crossed staff*

(FIG. 4) *On a staff in a group of other flags*

(FIG. 5) *With flags of other nations*

When the flag is displayed in a window, the field of stars should be displayed in the same way (to the left as seen by someone outside).

In a procession with other flags (FIG. 2), the Stars and Stripes should be carried either to the marchers' right in a line of flags or to the front and center of a line of other flags (top right).

When the Stars and Stripes and another flag are displayed on crossed staffs (FIG. 3), the Stars and Stripes should be on the right (observer's left) and its staff should be placed in front.

Displayed on a staff in a group of other flags from various states, localities, or societies (FIG. 4), the U. S. flag should always be at the center and highest point.

When the flags of several nations are flown together (FIG. 5), they should wave from an equal height. The U. S. flag should fly to the right of the others (observer's left). The Stars and Stripes should be hoisted first and lowered last.

The flag should always fly free, never touching anything beneath it. It should never be used as wearing apparel, drapery, or bedding. Red-white-and-blue bunting should be used for decorative purposes such as draping for a speaker's platform; the bunting should be hung with the blue stripe at the top, white in the middle, and red below.

The flag should never be used for advertising purposes, embroidered on cushions or handkerchiefs, or reproduced on any goods designed for temporary use and disposal.

When the flag is weatherworn or otherwise damaged so that it is no longer fit for display, it should be destroyed in a dignified manner, preferably by burning.

Index

Boldface indicates illustrations.

Italic indicates captions.

A young patriot wears a hat decorated with the Stars and Stripes.

Shriners maneuver their out-of-scale cars in Rowley, Iowa's Fourth of July parade.

*Dressing to extremes, two starry-eyed
Vermonters celebrate the Fourth of July.*

Illustrations Credits

Cover, William J. Hebert/Getty Images; Portfolio: Ethan Miller /Reuters NewMedia, Inc./Corbis; Grant V. Faint/Getty Images; Steven Hirsch/Corbis Sygma; David Sanders/Arizona Daily Star; Beth A. Keiser/AFP/Corbis; Mark Peterson /Corbis SABA; Michael Macor/SF Chronicle/Corbis SABA; Brennan Linsley /AURORA; James Nachtwey/VII.

INTRODUCTION: 10, THE PEALE MUSEUM, Baltimore City Life Museums. 12, THE BETTMANN ARCHIVE. 13, Mary Motley Kalergis. 14, Jerry Mesner/FOLIO, INC. 15, Baron Wolman. 16, WALTERS ART GALLERY, Baltimore. 17, MARYLAND HISTORICAL SOCIETY, Baltimore. 18-19, L. Kenneth Townsend/NATIONAL PARK SERVICE. 20, CULVER PICTURES, INC. 22, MARYLAND HISTORICAL SOCIETY, Baltimore. 22, THE PEALE MUSEUM, Baltimore City Life Museums/Hambleton Collection. 23, THE PEALE MUSEUM, Baltimore City Life Museums. 25, SMITHSONIAN INSTITUTION, Photo #83.7221.

CHAPTER 1: 26, THE GRANGER COLLECTION, New York. 28, Robert E. Hynes. 29, STATE CAPITOL, Commonwealth of Virginia. 30, Robert E. Hynes. 32-33, John Trumbull, "The Death of General Warren at the Battle of Bunker's Hill, 17 June 1775," YALE UNIVERSITY ART GALLERY/Trumbull Collection. 34 left, Robert E. Hynes. 34 right, Courtesy BEDFORD FREE PUBLIC LIBRARY. 35 left, THE LIBRARY COMPANY OF PHILADELPHIA. 35 right (both), Robert E. Hynes. 36, Robert E. Hynes. 37 top, THE BETTMANN ARCHIVE. 37 bottom, Robert E. Hynes. 38, SMITHSONIAN INSTITUTION/Courtesy of the Board of Education, Somerville, MA. 40-41, engraving by John C. McRae after a painting by F. A. Charman, LIBRARY OF CONGRESS. 42, 43, Robert E. Hynes. 44 top, THE GRANGER COLLECTION, New York. 44 bottom, Robert E. Hynes. 45, HISTORICAL SOCIETY OF PENNSYLVANIA. 46, painting by Ferdinand de Brackeleer, Collection of Hugh S. Watson, Jr. 47, CHICAGO HISTORICAL SOCIETY. 48-49, Robert Llewellyn. 50 top left, FORT TICONDEROGA MUSEUM. 50 top right, NORTH CAROLINA DIVISION OF ARCHIVES & HISTORY. 50 bottom left, Courtesy EASTON AREA PUBLIC LIBRARY/Steve Winter Photographer. 50 bottom right, from the collection of THE BENNINGTON MUSEUM, Bennington, Vermont. 51, from the collection of LOUISIANA STATE MUSEUM. 53, Charles Shoffner.

CHAPTER 2: 54, Joe Rosenthal/WIDE WORLD PHOTOS, INC. 56, October 31, 1765/HISTORICAL SOCIETY OF PENNSYLVANIA. 57, THE BETTMANN ARCHIVE. 58, © painting "Drafting of the Declaration of Independence," by J.L.G. Ferris/SMITHSONIAN INSTITUTION. 59, THE GRANGER COLLECTION, New York. 60-61, CAPITOL ART COLLECTION. 62 both, THE BETTMANN ARCHIVE. 63, THE GRANGER COLLECTION, New York. 64-65, THE GRANGER COLLECTION, New York. 66, Courtesy AMON CARTER MUSEUM/Fort Worth, Texas. 67, THE GRANGER COLLECTION, New York. 68 top, NAVAL HISTORICAL CENTER. 68 bottom, B.A. Stewart/Japanese print from the Chadbourne Collection, LIBRARY OF CONGRESS. 69 top, CULVER PICTURES, INC. 69 bottom left, Japanese print from the Chadbourne Collection, LIBRARY OF CONGRESS. 69 bottom right, U.S. NAVAL ACADEMY MUSEUM. 70, CHICAGO HISTORICAL SOCIETY, ICHi-22044. 71, Eleanor S. Brockenbrough Library, MUSEUM OF THE CONFEDERACY, Richmond, VA/Katherine Wetzel Photo. 72-73, LIBRARY OF CONGRESS. 74 top, Lloyd Ostendorf/Dayton, Ohio. 74 bottom, U.S. ARMY MILITARY HISTORY INSTITUTE. 75 left (all), MUSEUM OF THE CONFEDERACY, Richmond, VA/Katherine Wetzel Photo. 75 right, William A. Turner, LaPlata, MD. 76, Courtesy CHICAGO HISTORICAL SOCIETY. 77, LIBRARY OF CONGRESS. 78, SMITHSONIAN INSTITUTION. 78-79, National Anthropological Archives/SMITHSONIAN INSTITUTION. 79, Darryl Lyons Collection, Mayfield Heights, OH. 80, THE BETTMANN ARCHIVE. 81, THE GRANGER COLLECTION, New York. 82, BROWN BROTHERS, Sterling, PA. 83, NATIONAL ARCHIVES. 84 top, MARY EVANS PICTURE LIBRARY. 84 bottom, THE GRANGER COLLECTION, New York. 85 left, COMSTOCK, INC. 85 top right, THE GRANGER COLLECTION, New York. 85 bottom right, THE BETTMANN ARCHIVE. 86-87, PHOTOWORLD/FPG INT'L. 88, THE BETTMAN ARCHIVE. 89 top, CULVER PICTURES, INC. 89 bottom, Othroyaki Matsumoto/BLACK STAR. 90, Kelso Daly/LIFE MAGAZINE © TIME WARNER INC. 91 top, UNITED STATES ARMY. 91 bottom, THE BETTMANN ARCHIVE. 92-93, THE BETTMANN ARCHIVE. 94 left, ARCHIV/PHOTO RESEARCHERS, INC.

94 top right, LIBRARY OF CONGRESS. 94 bottom right, Chronicle Pictures, Inc./PHOTO RESEARCHERS, INC. 95, CULVER PICTURES, INC. 96, THE BETTMANN ARCHIVE. 97, U.S. ARMY AIR FORCES, Official. 98, CULVER PICTURES, INC. 99, NATIONAL ARCHIVES. 100, Werner Wolff/BLACK STAR. 101, Elliott Erwitt/ MAGNUM. 102, Robert Caputo. 103, David C. Boyer. 104, THE BETTMANN ARCHIVE. 104-05, Robert Ellison/BLACK STAR. 106, AP/ WIDE WORLD PHOTOS. 107, Bernie Boston. 108, Vince Mannino/UPI-THE BETTMANN ARCHIVE. 109, Peter Marbottom/MAGNUM. 110, Wally McNamee/WOODFIN CAMP & ASSOC. 110-111, Larry Downing/WOODFIN CAMP & ASSOC. 112-113, Abbas/MAGNUM. 113, David Turnley, DETROIT FREE PRESS/BLACK STAR. 115, Les Stone/ SYGMA. 117, Jake Rajs.

CHAPTER 3: 118, NASA/Eugene A. Cernan. 120. THE GRANGER COLLECTION, New York. 120-121, David Muench. 122-123, OREGON STATE CAPITOL ROTUNDA, SALEM/James A. Sugar, Photographer. 124 both, Charles Willson Peale, 1807, 1810/ INDEPENDENCE NATIONAL HISTORICAL PARK COLLECTION, Philadelphia. 125, Courtesy THOMASSON-GRANT, INC. 126 both, MISSOURI HISTORICAL SOCIETY, St. Louis. 127 top, NATIONAL ARCHIVES. 127 bottom (both), Marie Nonnast Bohlen. 128-129, Courtesy of the MONTANA HISTORICAL SOCIETY. 130, INDEPENDENCE NATIONAL HISTORICAL PARK COLLECTION. 131, Jake Rajs. 132-133, David Muench. 134, CULVER PICTURES, INC. 135 left, HISTORICAL PICTURES SERVICE, Chicago. 135 right, Courtesy of the SOUTHWEST MUSEUM, Los Angeles, photo # CT. 9. 136, Yale Collection of Western Americana, BEINECKE RARE BOOK AND MANUSCRIPT LIBRARY. 137, NAVAL HISTORY MUSEUM. 138-139, D. Parer & E. Parer-Cook/ AUSCAPE INTERNATIONAL. 140 both SMITHSONIAN INSTITUTION, photo #68356, #68355. 141, J. K. Hillers/ U.S.G.S. 142 top, BROWN BROTHERS, Sterling, PA. 142 bottom, engraving from "Canyons of the Colorado" by J.W. Powell, published 1895 by Flood and Vincent/Walter Meayers Edwards Photographer. 143 top, Tom Till. 143 bottom, J.K. Hillers/U.S.G.S. 144 left, CULVER PICTURES, INC. 144 right, THE GRANGER COLLECTION, New York. 145, Robert Caputo. 146, THE BETTMANN ARCHIVE. 147 top and bottom, Adm. Robert E. Peary. 148, Adm. Robert E. Peary. 149 top and bottom right, Adm. Robert E. Peary. 149 bottom left, Robert S. Oakes. 150-151, painting by N.C. Wyeth for NATIONAL GEOGRAPHIC. 152, BYRD ANTARCTIC EXPEDITION. 153, Courtesy of PARAMOUNT PUBLIC CORPORATION. 154, Barry C. Bishop/NATIONAL GEOGRAPHIC Staff. 155, Nawang Gomba. 156 top, Al Giddings. 156 bottom, John Tee-Van. 157, Emory Kristof/ NATIONAL GEOGRAPHIC Photographer, Michael Cole, and Keith A. Moorehead. 158, NASA Photo courtesy of JAMES LONG ASSOCIATES. 159, NASA. 160, NASA. 160-161, NASA/JET PROPULSION LAB. 163, NASA.

CHAPTER 4: 164, Courtesy of the NEW-YORK HISTORICAL SOCIETY, N.Y.C. 166, PHOTOWORLD/FPG INT'L. 166-167, Frank Siteman/STOCK, BOSTON. 168, PHOTOWORLD/FPG INT'L. 169, William Albert Allard. 170 top, Gianni Giansanti/SYGMA. 170 bottom, © ALLSPORT/ Mike Hewitt, 1993. 171, © ALLSPORT/Mike Powell, 1993. 172-173, James C. Richardson. 174, Joseph Paulicek/MINNESOTA HISTORICAL SOCIETY. 175, NEW YORK STATE HISTORICAL ASSOCIATION, Cooperstown. 176 top, Courtesy of Frank P. Di Berardino. 176 bottom, Ted Wood. 177, THE BETTMANN ARCHIVE. 178, CULVER PICTURES, INC. 179, F.B. Grunzweig/PHOTO RESEARCHERS, INC. 180, BROWN BROTHERS, Sterling, PA. 180-181, THE GRANGER COLLECTION, New York. 182, Stanley J. Forman/Pulitzer Prize 1976. 183, Dan Budnik/WOODFIN CAMP & ASSOC. 185, Courtesy of the WITKIN GALLERY, INC., New York City. 186-187, CULVER PICTURES, INC. 188, CULVER PICTURES, INC. 189, "PATTON" © 1970 TWENTIETH CENTURY FOX FILM CORPORATION. All Rights Reserved. 190, THE GRANGER COLLECTION, New York. 191, John Nieto Painting/Courtesy J. CACCIOLA GALLERY. 192, Dennis Cowley, Photographer/Courtesy MAX PROTETCH GALLERY, New York. 193, © Jasper Johns/VAGA, New York 1993. Collection of WHITNEY MUSEUM OF AMERICAN ART, New York. Photography by Geoffrey Clements, N.Y. 194 top, David J. Carol /THE IMAGE BANK. 194 bottom, Collection MUSEUM OF AMERICAN FOLK ART, Gift of Herbert Waide Hemphill, Jr./Seth Joel Photographer. 195 top, Collection MUSEUM OF AMERICAN FOLK ART, Promised bequest of Dorothy and Leo Rabkin. 195 bottom, Collection MUSEUM OF AMERICAN FOLK ART, Gift of Phyllis Haders. 196, George F. Mobley, NATIONAL GEOGRAPHIC Photographer. 197, Cameron Davidson/FOLIO, INC. 198-199, Ted Wood. 200 left, Pete Turner/THE IMAGE BANK. 200 right, Tom Tracy/THE STOCK MARKET. 201 top, Michael Ventura/BRUCE

COLEMAN INC. 201 bottom, Pete Turner/THE IMAGE BANK. 202, UNDERWOOD & UNDERWOOD. 203, © 1991 Michael Montfort/MICHAEL OCHS ARCHIVES/Venice, CA. 204, Tony Ray Jones/MAGNUM. 205, Burk Uzzle. 206-207, Harlan A. Marshall. 208, THE BETTMAN ARCHIVE. 209, John Strickler/THE MERCURY/Pottstown, PA. 210 top, UPI/THE BETTMAN ARCHIVE. 210 bottom, Henry Diltz. 211 both, Jacques Chenet/WOODFIN CAMP & ASSOC. 212, Theodore Roosevelt Photograph By R.Y. Young, LIBRARY OF CONGRESS. 213, WIDE WORLD PHOTOS. 214-215, Joseph Sohm/CHROMOSOHM. 216 top, Olivier Rebbot/ WOODFIN CAMP & ASSOC. 216 bottom, THE GRANGER COLLECTION, New York. 217 top left, THE GRANGER COLLECTION, New York. 217 bottom left, Victor Boswell/NATIONAL GEOGRAPHIC Photographer. 217 center right, THE GRANGER COLLECTION, New York. 217 bottom, Leonard G. Phillips. 218-219, Scott Andrews. 220-221, Jake Rajs. 223, Tom Sanders. 224 top, Joseph Sohm/ CHROMOSOHM. 224 bottom, Jim Richardson/WESTLIGHT. 225 all, Robert E. Hynes. 227, Dan Dry. 228, George Olson/ WOODFIN CAMP & ASSOC. 230, Susan Lapides/WOODFIN CAMP & ASSOC. 232, Annie Griffiths Belt.

Library of Congress CIP Data

Sedeen, Margaret.
   Star-Spangled Banner : our nation and its flag / by Margaret Sedeen : prepared by the Book Division, National Geographic Society.
      p.   cm.
   Includes index.
   ISBN 0-87044-944-3. -- ISBN 0-87044-945-1 (deluxe)
   1. Flags--United States--History.   I. National Geographic Society (U. S.). Book Division.   II. Title.
CR113.S4   1993
929.9'2--dc20   93-15173
                                                        CIP

The Francis Scott Key Foundation has created the Star-Spangled Banner Monument located at Key Bridge in Washington, D.C. Through its educational programs and The Honor America! Roll, a computerized registry of patriotic Americans, the Foundation celebrates the legacy of an American hero whose commitment to the ideals and responsibilities of democracy serves as a model for us all. Tax-deductible contributions may be sent to the following address: The Francis Scott Key Foundation
P.O. Box 90015, Washington, D.C. 20069-0015

With special thanks to Richard H. Rovsek, Chairman, and Richard Allen, President, American Marketing and Events, Santa Barbara, California.

Copyright © 1993, 2001 National Geographic Society. All rights reserved. Reproduction of the whole or any part of the contents without written permission is prohibited.

Baseball players salute Old Glory.